HUMPTY DUMPTY

BY ERIC BOGOSIAN

★

★

DRAMATISTS
PLAY SERVICE
INC.

HUMPTY DUMPTY
Copyright © 2005, Eric Bogosian

All Rights Reserved

SPECIAL NOTE

SPECIAL NOTE ON SONGS AND RECORDINGS

HUMPTY DUMPTY premiered at The McCarter Theater in Princeton, New Jersey, on March 29, 2002, directed by Jo Bonney.

NICOLE .... Kathryn Meisle
MAX .... Bruce Norris
TROY .... Patrick Fabian
SPOON .... Reiko Aylesworth
NAT .... Michael Laurence

A revised version of the play was produced at the San Jose Repertory Theatre in San Jose, California, on March 28, 2003, directed by John McLuggage.

NICOLE .... Elizabeth Hanley Rice
MAX .... Saxon Palmer
TROY .... Louis Lotorto
SPOON .... Amy Brewczynski
NAT .... Andy Murray

HUMPTY DUMPTY

ACT ONE

Scene 1

Late afternoon light pours into a roomy vacation home that had once been a barn. Comfy armchairs, a couch and an oak table face an enormous bluestone fireplace. Elevated about two feet above the rest of the space is the kitchen, behind which a windowpane door leads out to a glassed-in "mud room" porch and out of doors. The rest of the spacious room is furnished with collectible pottery, mission armchairs, bookcases and kilim throw rugs. An upstage balcony leads to three bedrooms. Nicole enters from outside, wrestling luggage and groceries. She is on her cell phone. Her tone is clipped and brash.

NICOLE. *(To phone.)* Right. Uh-huh. No, business class is fine, I don't need first. But get me priority check-in no matter what. And did you give them the frequent flyer number? Oh shit, you're breaking up ... damn! *(Nicole unloads groceries and finds a "good spot" for the cell as Max arrives with a case of books.)* No there, OK. You ordered the special meal? What? No. That's *not* the same.

No, cheese is *not* the same as tofu, Sara. Tell them it has to be *totally* non-dairy. And make sure they have bottled water. If not ... Hold on, Sara. *(To Max.)* What?

MAX. I can't find my laptop.

NICOLE. It's on your shoulder. *(To phone:)* We just got here. Literally just walked in. It's nice. It's ...

MAX.
Did you take my laptop out of the car?

MAX.
(Sees it.) Oh, right.

(Max drops the box of books and heads back out for luggage. Nicole wanders.)

NICOLE. *(To phone:)* ... a little weird. But I guess all new places are weird. That's the definition of weird, isn't it? So Sara? Call the car company, put the confirmation number on my voice mail and maybe I'll talk to you tomorrow. Hello? What? OK. Bye. *(Max returns with more luggage. He's so overwhelmed with stuff, he hasn't even looked around at the place.)*

MAX. I think I got everything. Fuck. *(Max drops onto the couch, exhausted. Nicole clicks off and flops down next to him. Suddenly stillness fills the air. A chickadee is chirping somewhere.)*

NICOLE. Here we are! A mere five and a half hours later.

MAX. I need drugs.

NICOLE. This *is* drugs. Just more expensive. *(Restless, Max jumps up to inventory what they've got.)*

MAX. So ... Cable with HBO. Three working fireplaces. Views. Lots of views. Cedar Jacuzzi for two. And let's not forget the fully-equipped chef's kitchen. *(Checking.)* Stove doesn't light. Not to mention nearby walking paths and pastoral pond with gazebo. All in a life-affirming, isolated picturesque setting far from the madding crowd. *(As Max opens cabinets and closets, Nicole has wandered upstairs and begins to explore the bedrooms.)*

NICOLE. *(Off.)* Lots of quilts and handmade pottery. Macrame wall-hangings. Fireplaces in each bedroom. Cedar Jacuzzi.

MAX. I said that already. I said cedar Jacuzzi.

NICOLE. *(Still off.)* No cable up here. And no fax machine anywhere. Cell phone barely works. And how do we do e-mail?

MAX. We don't. That's the point. For one week, we don't do anything. No faxes. No e-mail.

NICOLE. *(Returning:)* How much did all this rustic splendor cost? *(Seeing it:)* Espresso machine.

MAX. Three grand. Plus complimentary ski lift tickets.

NICOLE. It's too early for snow, isn't it?

MAX. That's why they're complimentary. *(Nicole hugs Max, kisses him, then moves off again.)*

NICOLE. You did good. I prefer Saint Bart's, but like you said, this way we avoid airports, lines, X-ray machines. No delays, no terrorists. Just downtime. Good old-fashioned downtime.

MAX. Plus the Caribbean is so, you know, *Nineties.* Monotonous white beaches, everything stinking of sunblock. Third-world service personnel grinning and shuffling, trying to guilt you out for being

6

American. You have to stay drunk and play golf and tennis all day long just to stave off the boredom. I *hate* golf and tennis.

NICOLE. You left out snorkeling in the blue-green water.

MAX. Fuck the blue-green water! The whole thing smacks of decadence and colonialism. This is much better, healthier, more patriotic even. We'll go for hikes. We'll rock-climb. We'll contemplate nature. We'll breathe pure oxygen.

NICOLE. *Cold* pure oxygen. Where's the thermostat?

MAX. No wait, lemme make a fire. If we're going to do this, let's do it right. *(Nicole searches shelves as Max works at the fireplace.)*

NICOLE. Jigsaw puzzles. Scrabble. Hmmmm. *Art and Antiques, House and Garden, American Quilting!* Oh my, *The Joy of Sex!*

MAX. There you go! See? We'll try out new erotic positions on a bear-skin rug! *(Max finds a note on the mantle.)* A note! *(Nicole finds the record player and a box of records as Max reads the note out loud:)* "Trash day is Tuesday. Be sure to fasten the lids tightly or the raccoons *will* get in. Keep thermostat on sixty-eight. Don't flush tampons or other foreign objects down the toilet." Foreign objects?! "Feel free to use the homemade peanut butter." *What?!* Emergency numbers ... Yada. Yada. "Extra quilts in the cupboard." This place is the quilt mecca. Oh, and this is in bold: "There's no smoking of any kind." And I just bought that new crack pipe! "Have a great time! Ted and Sondra!" Well, they sound like loads of fun. *(Max lights the paper under the wood in the fireplace.)*

NICOLE. Check out this vinyl! Jethro Tull. Joan Baez. Van Morrison. I bet they went to Woodstock. *(Nicole puts a record on: maybe "Moondance" by Van Morrison.* Max steps back as the fireplace comes to life.)*

MAX. Voilà! *(Nicole wraps her arms around Max.)*

NICOLE. You did that so well! A regular frontiersman. I'm impressed. My own Daniel Boone. *(Entwined, Nicole and Max watch the fire.)* How 'bout this? Since I am ovulating right this very second, why don't we put all these quilts and sex books to work and get me pregnant!

MAX. Troy and Spoon are going to be here any minute.

NICOLE. We'll have a quickie. "Wham. Bam. Thank you, ma'am."

MAX. I'm not that kind of guy.

NICOLE. Every guy is that kind of guy. *(She rubs his shoulders.)* You're very tense. You need to relax.

MAX. I'm relaxed.

NICOLE. No you're not.

MAX. I'm in the country aren't I? I mean, how much more relaxed can I get? Maybe I should go out and chop down a tree?

NICOLE. *(Nuzzling him.)* C'mon, let's fuck.

MAX. Nicole, you're undercutting my need to obsess.

NICOLE. *(More nuzzling.)* What are you obsessed about?

MAX. Everything. Money, my novel, selling the book, selling out, money. Pretty much money.

NICOLE. Don't you want to get me pregnant?

MAX. Of course I do. *(They start kissing. Nicole takes Max's hand.)*

NICOLE. Time to pack all that anxiety away. Time to become obsessed with *me.* Who knows? We might relax and start enjoying ourselves. Come on, Davy Crockett, you can make another fire upstairs.

MAX. I thought I was Daniel Boone. *(They begin to move up the steps. Kiss. They laugh like kids. Hands all over each other. Max is stripping her clothes off. They're at the top of the steps, and enter the room. The phone rings. Nicole reemerges in a teddy and panties and calls back over her shoulder:)*

NICOLE. I just want to listen and see who it is.

MAX. *(Off.)* Nicole!

NICOLE. Only take a sec.

MAX. *(Off.)* Who'd you give this number to?

NICOLE. No one. Well, Billy, but that's because … *(The answering machine kicks in.)*

MESSAGE MACHINE VOICE. *(Woman's voice.)* Hello, this is Ted and Sondra. *(Guy's voice:)* Hi! *(Woman:)* We're not here right now, so leave a message. If not, have a great 24/7! *(BEEP.)*

VOICE. *(Billy.)* Nicole? It's Billy. We have a little problem …

NICOLE. … we were on deadline and …

BILLY.	MAX.
The author wants a note re: the typeface and we didn't figure that into the page count, so the books won't break out evenly. He's really adamant about it. In fact, now he says he wants the acknowldgements …	You gave your copy editor this number?

NICOLE.
I had to.
MAX.
Well, call him back later. *(Nicole is moving toward the phone.)* |

NICOLE. I can't, it has to be done by Monday. *(Nicole picks up. To phone.)* Hey. It's me. No, nothing Billy, just hanging out. What's up? Uh-huh. *(Max has come down to join her. Thinking it won't be a long call, he caresses her as she listens to Billy. Nicole waves Max away. He stands a few feet off, waiting.)* Uh-huh. Uh-huh. OK. OK. OK. No. Just a sec, Billy. *(To Max.)* Go make your fire! I'll be right up. *(Max makes a sign to "hurry up" and turns, goes up the stairs. Goes into the bedroom.)* Yeah. Well, listen Billy, that's the way it is. He just has to deal with it. No. I can't call him now. I can't. Just do it, I don't care. So OK. OK? Huh? Sara? I guess, put her on. *(Nicole looks up to see that Max is gone. She starts pulling off her half-stockings.)* What? No, I can't take a *cab!* What happened to the car service? *(Beat.)* Oh, fuck them. I always have a car when I get to O'Hare, and that's it. Just make it happen. *(A man, Nat, can be seen entering the mud room. He observes Nicole for a moment as she talks, before rapping on the glass.)* Just a sec, Sara. *(Startled.)* Hello? *(Nicole grabs Max's jacket, which is lying nearby, slips it on.)*
NAT. I work for the Murphys?
NICOLE. Who?
NAT. The Murphys? Ted and Sondra?
NICOLE. Oh. Right. *(Calling out:)* MAX?!
NAT. Mind if I…?
NICOLE. *(Standing:)* No, no, come on in. MAX?
NAT. *(Entering:)* I'm sorry. I, uh, I just wanted to say hello. My name's Nat. I look after the house. You're the guests?
NICOLE. Yes. Right. Nat. Nice to meet you. I'm Nicole. *(Max appears in the bedroom door in his boxers pulling on a shirt.)*
MAX. Is that them?
NICOLE. No, it's "Nat." Works for the Murphys. *(To phone:)* Oh Sara? Just a sec.
MAX. Who are "the Murphys"?
NICOLE. *(To Max:)* The people we rented the house from?
MAX. *(To Nicole.)* Oh right. *(Max disappears back in the room. Nicole holds one finger up to Nat, as in "one sec.")*
NICOLE. *(To phone:)* OK, so. Do that. And see if you can upgrade to a suite. And don't forget I have to be at least three rooms away from the ice machine. *(Max reappears fully dressed and trots down the stairs, seeing Nat for the first time. To phone:)* Just tell them, Sara. They'll figure it out.
NAT. *(To Max.)* Ted said I should look at the stove.
MAX. Oh, right. *(Nat steps over to the stove and flicks on one of the*

9

burners. Max gives a panicky look to Nicole as Nat gets engrossed in the stove.)

NICOLE. *(To Max:)* I'm going upstairs. Hang it up for me? *(Nicole moves upstairs and into a bedroom.)*

MAX. You know it's no big deal, why don't you just leave it?

NAT. Oh, no, no. If your stove doesn't work, how you gonna eat?

NICOLE. *(Off.)* OK! *(Max hangs up the phone. Nat tinkers with the stove.)*

MAX. It won't light. But I can use matches.

NAT. Not a problem at all. Just needs an adjustment. *(Beat. Max watches Nat tinker.)*

MAX. So. Think we'll get snow?

NAT. Sooner or later.

MAX. I better check the *Old Farmer's Almanac*, eh? *(Nat is contorting himself over the top of the stove.)*

NAT. Or the Weather Channel. Say, hand me that socket wrench there?

MAX. Sure thing. This one? *(Hands him a wrench.)*

NAT. The socket wrench. There.

MAX. Oh, right.

NAT. *(Taking it.)* Thanks. *(Impotently, Max watches Nat work. Nicole comes out to the landing, looks down.)*

NICOLE. Max? *(Max steps over to look up to Nicole, shrugs. Gives her the one minute sign. Nicole goes back inside the bedroom.)*

MAX. Uh, so where do we go around here for groceries?

NAT. Well, you got milk, bread, soda, Lotto tickets down at the gas station on Mason Hill Road. Need anything fancy, you gotta go down the turnpike a way, where the Wal-Mart is.

MAX. That's a trip. Must be twenty miles.

NAT. Uh-huh. *(Nat drops a piece of the stove top onto his finger. Reacting.)* Owww! Cheese Louise! *(In the mud room, Troy and Spoon appear, lugging travel bags, groceries. Troy dressed in Dolce & Gabbana. Spoon in Prada "country attire." Max rushes to the back door, opening it.)*

TROY. *(Entering, on cell:)* ... his notes were OK. Predictable, but OK. He wants a female angle so I'll lay in a love interest ... *(Max backs up and shouts up to the balcony.)*

MAX. NICOLE! They're here!

TROY. ... ramp up the confrontation with his dad before act three and he'll buy it. *(Max hugs Spoon as Troy rolls in, finishing his call.)*

MAX. *(To Troy:)* You're here! Didn't expect you so early! *(To Spoon.)* Hi!

10

SPOON. You told Troy five hours, so he had to make it in four. Did ninety all the way.

TROY. *(To cell:)* Look, I'm here. I should jump. But tell him the fifty thousand as production bonus is a deal breaker. Just do it, Keith. *(Turning to Max:)* Maximilian! *(Hugs Max.)* Hey man! Look at you! *(Max and Troy hug. Nicole emerges from the bedroom, fully dressed. Spoon takes in the place.)*

SPOON. This place is amazing! What is it? A barn?

MAX. I guess so, yeah. A New Age barn.

SPOON. I *love* this! *(Looking around.)* It's like we're in the middle of nowhere! Troy, this is like Bobby's place in Montana.

MAX. Thirty-five acres surrounded by one thousand square miles of state forest. This area hasn't changed since the eighteenth century.

NICOLE?!

TROY. Bobby has over three hundred acres.

NICOLE. Troy! Hi! Hi! Spoon! Max, help them with their stuff!

NAT. Lemme give you a hand there. *(Troy, Max and Nat go out as Nicole comes downstairs.)*

SPOON. Hi Nicole!

NICOLE. You made it!

SPOON. Barely! Delayed in L.A., delayed in New York. I thought we'd never land. *(Troy and Max return hauling cartons and bags.)*

TROY. They wanted to strip-search Spoon. Full body cavity inspection. I had to threaten them with a pair of fingernail clippers.

SPOON. Stoppit. They made me take off my shoes! I mean, duh, like I'm going to blow up the plane with my shoes, right.

NICOLE. *(To Troy, double-kiss.)* Hi. Hi. All this food! Did you happen to bring any soy milk, Troy?

TROY. Soy-milk, no. *But* I did discover a mind-blowing Australian Shiraz and two Napa Pinot Grigios that are indistinguishable from mother's milk. And check this out, '92 Haut Brion. Two hundred and fifty dollars a bottle. *(Troy turns to Nat hauling in a cooler.)* How you doin'? I'm Troy, by the way. This is Spoon.

NAT. Hi. Uh "Spoon"?

SPOON. Spoon. As in tea*spoon,* table*spoon.* Cutlery. My parents were hippies. It's short for spoonful.

NAT. OK. *(Spoon grows shy before Nat's gaze. She turns to Troy.)*

SPOON. My hair's weird. Is my hair weird?

MAX. Nat's here doing some work.

SPOON. Wow, cool! You're a writer too?

NAT. No. No. Just, you know, fixing the stove.

SPOON. Really? I've always wanted to be able to do that, you know, fix things. *(Max is into the groceries, Nat returns to the stove.)*
MAX. Edamame, good. Belgian butter. And we got the jumbo shrimp.
SPOON. Not farm shrimp, Max! I can't eat anything raised on antibiotics or hormones. *(Spoon zips up the steps. Max calls up after her:)*
MAX. No, no. I think they're just big due to Darwinian selection. Survival-of-the-fittest shrimp.
TROY. Check out this off-the-hook focaccia! Ninety-year-old Italian lady on Elizabeth Street bakes it in an authentic stone oven her father built in 1910. *(Spoon calls out from the top of the stairs.)*
SPOON. Troy! This sunset, wow! The view is amazing!
TROY. *(Chewing.)* Nicole, come here!
NICOLE. What?
TROY. Open your mouth.
NICOLE. No. *(Nicole opens her mouth and Troy places an olive in her mouth. Spoon disappears into the rooms upstairs.)*
TROY. These are the olives the Greek gods ate on Mount Olympus. Ambrosial. Single-estate. The bomb.
NICOLE. M-mmmmm. Max, did you remember to get the little grape tomatoes?
MAX. I got the vine-ripened Dutch ones instead. Troy, when did you start talking this hip-hop lingo? You sound like P. Diddy on a bad day.
TROY. It's from hanging with studio executives. They feel better about paying me my quote when they're not quite sure what I'm saying. *(More food:)* Dig this cheese! Aged sheep's milk from, get this, *Kosovo!* How cool is that? And Armenian string cheese, the real stuff, not that shrink-wrapped supermarket dreck. Max, Max, Max — check out this caviar.
MAX. Caviar isn't yellow.
TROY. Oh yes it *is!* This, my friend, is "Sterlet." Formerly reserved for the Shah of Iran.
NICOLE. Caviar?
TROY. *(To Nat.)* Can't sip the Stoli without the fish eggs! *(Spoon is sailing in and out of the bedrooms.)*
SPOON. Fireplaces! And quilts! It's so nurturing!
NICOLE. Troy we're only here for the week.
TROY. That's what they said in Stalingrad!
MAX. This is known as conspicuous consumption.

12

TROY. Wrong! It takes discrimination, sophistication and skill to assemble this pile of goodies. It may be conspicuous, but it is not obvious.

MAX. Yellow caviar.

TROY. Listen, when you're gazing out at the purple mountains, imbibing the most impeccable armagnac, nibbling the silkiest brie on a slice of sun-ripened Normandy pear, when you are enjoying a singular and perfect moment in your life, you will thank me. *(Spoon has come back down the stairs, goes to a window.)*

NAT. Your stove's all set.

SPOON. Oh Troy, check out the deer, she's so cute! Just nibbling the bushes. Troy, look!

NAT. Oh you'll see everything up here: deer, coyote, wild turkey.

SPOON. That's so great!

NAT. S'posed to be mountain lion up on the ridge.

NICOLE. Aren't they extinct?

NAT. Might be, but something ate my dog and it wasn't a raccoon. *(Was that a joke? Max steps over to Nat.)*

MAX. Thanks a lot, man. *(Reaching into his pocket.)* What do I...?

NAT. Oh, no, no. No charge! Listen, that's my number over on the fireplace. Just gimme a ring you guys need anything.

MAX. Well, uh ... nice meeting you, Nat. *(Spoon beams at Nat as he leaves.)*

TROY. Wow. Right out of a Norman Rockwell painting.

SPOON. What a nice man!

MAX. Guess he keeps an eye on the place. Plows the drive, rakes the leaves, like that.

TROY. Wrestles mountain lions.

NICOLE. No wonder he's in such good shape.

MAX. He's authentic, that's all. Not full of attitude like us urban-types. Just does his thing.

SPOON. It's kind of Zen-like.

TROY. "Authentic"? How?

MAX. Real. Genuine.

TROY. How is that guy more genuine than you or me?

MAX. You know what I'm saying. He doesn't seek validation from abstract achievement — money, kudos, a place in the pecking order. There is no pecking order in his life, there's no hierarchy out here. He just deals with the bare necessities. Eats, works, sleeps. Lives.

NICOLE. You don't know that.

MAX. Come on. Look at him. He's a totally centered human being.

13

Somebody who knows who he is. Unpretentious. Clear-minded.

SPOON. I see it. He's off the grid in every way.

NICOLE. That is a large pot of simmering crap.

MAX. Hey, all I know is I'd love to have that guy's life! Just dealing with the bare necessities. Keeping it simple. No mental static. No bullshit.

SPOON. I am so with you, Max.

TROY. No, you know what? You're right. It must be *so* rewarding. Driving an old truck. Making a big five bucks an hour. Doing yardwork for a living. Being illiterate. Having sex with the sheep. Ba-a-a-a-ah!

SPOON. *(Laughing.)* Troy! You so suck!

MAX. Troy, you know what you're problem is? You are totally parochial. You think the world begins at Morton's and ends at the Penisula Club.

TROY. Doesn't it? So ... listen we have to make a big decision: Shiraz or ... Champagne? *(Spoon's cell phone rings.)*

SPOON. *(To phone.)* Hello? Brian! Hi honey. Great. Huh? Where? L.A.? But I just got here! *(Nicole's cell phone rings.)*

NICOLE. *(Picking up, to cell.)* Yeah? Uh-huh. What are you telling me, Billy? *(Troy's cell phone rings.)*

SPOON. *(To cell.)* Well, because I'm on *vacation!* Oh, I can barely hear you!

TROY. *(To cell.)* Yo! Dog! Hey!!! Good. Good. Kicking back. Hanging with my homies. S'up? Uh-huh ... *(Troy goes to the back windows as he jots in his Palm Pilot.)*

NICOLE. *(To cell.)* But Billy, why can't you handle this?

SPOON. *(To phone.)* Can't I do it another time?

TROY. *(To cell.)* Keith, Keith, Keith, it's all solvable. No. Wait. Listen ... hello?

NICOLE. *(To cell.)* No, why do I have to talk to his agent? We have nothing to talk about.

SPOON. *(To cell.)* I want to do it. I do. But ... are you mad at me? Don't be mad at me.

NICOLE. *(To cell:)* Billy, I can't believe this hasn't been taken care of. NO. Do *not* give him this number.

TROY. *(To cell:)* Give him my number, I'll talk to him.

SPOON. *(Phone.)* Give me their number, I'll make it better.

NICOLE. *(To cell.)* Off course I'm pissed off. *Jesus,* Billy!

TROY. *(To cell.)* Alright, listen. I'll tell him I've always wanted to work with him, he's a great artist, I wrote the role for him, blah-

14

blah, woof-woof. OK? Keith, you worry too much.

NICOLE. *(To cell:) Billy,* the deadline has passed.

SPOON. *(Phone.)* I'm sorry. I'm a fuck up. I know. But I really can't. Tell them I'm sick. But I'd love to come on the show like maybe next month? OK? Is that going to be OK? *(Max's cell is silent. He checks it — nothing.)*

TROY. *(To cell:)* Keith, leave it to me. Just leave it. OK?

SPOON. *(To phone:)* Thank you. I love you too. I know you're only thinking of me. OK? OK.

NICOLE. *(To cell:)* Are you sure? No, don't tell me you're sure if you're not sure. OK. No. I said OK. Gotta go. *(Click.)*

SPOON. *(Phone:)* Gotta go. *(Click.)*

TROY. *(To cell:)* Gotta go. *(Click.)*

NICOLE. Fuck. If I'm not there, there's a total meltdown.

SPOON. My manager's pissed off at me.

MAX. Is that the thing you're doing at Paramount?

TROY. Nah, turned that in last week. That was the people at Interforce? They're producing my spec script. They go weak at the knees when they get on the phone with a star.

MAX. But I thought your spec was with Pressman?

NICOLE. You're writing *two* screenplays at the same time?

TROY. Three if you include the HBO thing, four if you include the production polish for Warner's. I'm like the guy with the spinning plates. Spin, spin, spin.

SPOON. *(Looks out the window.)* Oh look now there's a little rabbit! She *sees* us! She does! I wonder what she's thinking? *(Troy nuzzles Spoon from behind, kissing her neck.)*

TROY. She's thinking, I'm horny — where's Bugs?

SPOON. *(Coy.)* Yeah? *(Troy begins to kiss and fondle Spoon right in front of Nicole and Max. Max and Nicole ignore them. After a moment, Troy and Spoon "come out of it," obviously hungry for more ...)*

TROY. You know what, guys? We're going take our stuff up and unpack. *(Troy and Spoon grab up some luggage and skedaddle up to their room and slam the door. Nicole and Max are left with each other. Giggling behind the door.)*

MAX. Do you, uh, want to "unpack" too?

NICOLE. What?

MAX. Do you want to ... you know, go upstairs?

NICOLE. Uh ... maybe after dinner. You know? I don't think I can ... when they're ...

MAX. ... Right ...

NICOLE. … in the next room …

MAX. Right.

NICOLE. *(Beat.)* I should call Billy back. He's way over his depth.

MAX. Yeah.

NICOLE. Or not.

MAX. Whatever.

NICOLE. Let me just call him and then we'll unpack.

MAX. Good. *(Pause.)* I didn't realize Troy was doing so well. *(Nicole dials her cell. Max watches the rabbit out the window.)* I know what the rabbit is thinking.

NICOLE. *(Not really listening.)* What?

MAX. Why isn't my cell phone ringing?

Scene 2

Night. Troy, Nicole and Spoon sit by the fire playing Scrabble. Max is in the kitchen area, preparing desserts, the remains of dinner lay scattered. Dylan on the stereo.

MAX. It's all a function of American hegemony. I mean, the fucking IMF doesn't give a shit. They're happy to see the third world go down the tubes as long as we preserve the good life back home in the empire. Troy, did you see that picture last week in the *Times*? Little boy in the middle of a garbage dump outside Rio? Pathetic. Makes a living picking drinking straws out of the garbage.

NICOLE. *I* saw it. It made me nauseous!

MAX. Spoon, would you like the hazelnut torte or bittersweet chocolate mousse with raspberries?

SPOON. A little of both. What does he do with the drinking straws?

MAX. Oh, the kid? Washes them out and sells them to restaurants. Ten for a penny.

NICOLE. Probably why we got the raging shits in Tulum last year.

TROY. You should have told me you were in Tulum! I know the best little café, right on the beach. Just a shack, your toes are in sand while you eat.

SPOON. We're going to Puerto Vallarta in January.

TROY. You guys should come with us. Do a little fishing, a little

16

peyote, eat the worm in the bottle.

MAX. I can't believe you're on a vacation talking about your *next* vacation!

TROY. It's true. Sad but true. Nicole, are you digging this wine? Earthy, with just the barest hint of a blackberry finish. '82 Bordeaux, you can't beat it. Two glasses and it's like a week in Provence. *(Max joins the group with the desserts.)*

MAX. Actually it would be like a week in Bordeaux. Provence is a *region,* Bordeaux is a *city.* They're both in France, that's about all they have in common.

SPOON. Max, you know everything. Is Xanadu a word? *(Nicole pours herself another glass of wine.)*

NICOLE. "In Xanadu did Kubla Khan a stately pleasure-dome decree ... " et cetera, et cetera. The actual Xanadu was the summer palace of the Mongol royalty at Shangztu. And I think maybe Omar Khayyam had something to do with it.

MAX. Omar Khayyam wrote *The Rubaiyat,* Edward Fitzgerald translated it. Coleridge wrote "Xanadu." It's possible Fitzgerald and Coleridge knew each other. Same era, different generations.

SPOON. Oh. So I can use it?

TROY. It's not your turn. It's *my* turn.

SPOON. Troy! Be gentle, I've never done this before! *(Troy kisses her. They get into it. Nicole sips her wine.)*

NICOLE. Troy, this wine *is* nice.

TROY. Thank you, Spoon refuses to try it.

SPOON. That's not true! I'm just taking a little break from alcohol. Trying to realign, you know? Only spring water, tea and organic berry juice.

TROY. Spoon's concluded she's an alcoholic.

SPOON. I have done no such thing. I'm just not drinking.

TROY. Because you're afraid of losing control.

SPOON. I feel better this way. Serene.

TROY. Spoon believes in a perfect world where everyone meditates every day and eats no meat and where no animals are harmed ... ever. *(Laying tiles.)*

SPOON. I would love that world.

TROY. I'd be bored shitless in three days. *FUR-BISH.*

MAX. "Furbish." There's no such word! *Furbish?*

TROY. Of course there is. You *re-furbish* something, so you must be able to *furbish* it. Four, six, double word on the I — thirty. *(Spoon has picked up the dictionary.)*

SPOON. "Furbish: To brighten by cleaning or rubbing. To restore to attractive or serviceable condition. Renovate." You win, Troy. *(She kisses him.)*

TROY. Max, you may know everything, but I know more words. And have tighter abs.

SPOON. *(Moving tiles.)* "Xanadu." Fifteen. Oh! And I have a double word! Thirty!

MAX. *(Sulking.)* D-U. Not D-O-O.

NICOLE. Max. Relax, Max.

MAX. *(Huffy.)* "Wisdom." Fourteen. Double word. Twenty-eight. *(Moves tiles.)* We'll see who knows more words. You are all doomed. I am the Tiger Woods of Scrabble.

NICOLE. I met Tiger Woods last week. Nice guy. Sexy. *(Addressing her tiles:)* L-E-M-M-I-N-G "Lemming." Double letter on the M, and triple word — thirty-nine.

TROY. *(Troy makes a cursory glance at his tiles and quickly throws some down.)* Z-A-R-F. "Zarf." A holder, usually of ornamental metal, for a coffee cup. Double letter on the Z. Twenty-six. Hey, did you see Kurt's new novel already sold for a nice fat two mill?

NICOLE. Two point five. Binky cut the deal.

MAX. Well his last book was shit. "Zarf," huh?

TROY. Hey, I *like* Kurt's books. They're trashy and smart. *(Max gets up to find another bottle of wine.)*

MAX. Boutique intellectualism for the masses.

NICOLE. "The masses"?

MAX. The masses, the general public. All those average citizens who don't live in New York or L.A., and who read *People* magazine and watch the Oscars.

NICOLE. We read *People* magazine and watch the Oscars.

MAX. Yes, yes. But we do it *ironically.*

TROY. Well, it got him the Pulitzer.

MAX. So what?

TROY. Jealous?

MAX. I can't be jealous of an empty facade.

SPOON. Is it puh-litzer or pew-litzer?

TROY. I thought it's pooh-litzer.

SPOON. Max, I read your story in the *New Yorker*. I loved how you described that old man's thoughts. Like you were *so* inside his head! How do you do that?

MAX. Most people have an inner child. I have an inner geriatric.

SPOON. It was wonderful. I can't wait to read the whole book.

MAX. Thank you.

TROY. You should adapt it as a film!

NICOLE. He's going to. Max, didn't you tell Troy about the deal?

MAX. No, I …

NICOLE. Max just sold the option!

TROY. And you didn't tell me! Your best friend? When?

MAX. Two weeks ago. They took me out to lunch and they say they're going to buy it.

TROY. Lunch? Where? Bouley? Jean-Georges? Nobu?

MAX. I don't know, Troy! Someplace uptown. I wasn't paying any attention.

TROY. They're buying the book or just the option? And you're doing the screenplay? What are we talking about here? Six figures? Seven?

MAX. I don't know, Troy! I let the agents deal with all that.

TROY. Oh, we're being humble. Very endearing.

MAX. It's not about the money.

TROY. Of course it's not about the money. What is it about then? The art? C'mon, Max! You're dancing with the devil, you might as well enjoy yourself. Don't deny yourself the pleasure of gloating, you've been busting your ass for too long. *(Lifting his glass.)* A toast to Maxie: To paraphrase Oscar Wilde: "When I was young, I thought fame and fortune was everything. Now that I'm old, I *know* it is."

SPOON. Cheers!

ALL. Cheers! *(Nicole walks into the living room. Changes the music. Something like "Brown Sugar."* She dances to it. Troy begins to dance with her.)*

MAX. Spoon, what are *you* working on?

SPOON. Oh I might do this movie about Søren Kierkegaard? The existential philosopher? Very dark. According to the script he was really hung up on a girl named Regina. That's me.

MAX. A film about Søren Kierkegaard? Who's directing? *(Spoon gets up and starts dancing with Nicole and Troy.)*

SPOON. Spielberg. They're shooting in Copenhagen and everything.

MAX. Really? *(Miffed but not sure why.)* Spoon, it's your turn.

NICOLE. Max, come dance with me!

MAX. I thought we were playing … Spoon, it's your turn.

NICOLE. Max…! *(Troy floats by the table, grabs his wine, returns*

* See Special Note on Songs and Recordings on copyright page.

19

to the women, putting his arms around both of them. They love his playful energy.)

TROY. Say, why don't we have an orgy this weekend? Throw the car keys in a bowl? *(Nicole comes over to Max and leans over him.)*

NICOLE. I have a great word: J-I-G-G-Y.

MAX. That's not a word.

NICOLE. Sure it is. As in "jiggy-jiggy." *(Troy is dancing close to Spoon. They fall onto the couch and are smooching.)*

MAX. Anyway, it's not your turn. It's Spoon's turn. Spoon, come back to the table.

NICOLE. I'll take her turn.

MAX. You can't do that! *(Nicole and Max struggle slightly and she jogs the table.)* Now it's all fucked up! It's ruined! *(Nicole plops down into Max's lap. Giddy:)*

NICOLE. Hi.

MAX. I was winning! I had a great word.

NICOLE. I *know* you did, baby. *(The lights go out. The TV set blinks off, music cuts.)*

MAX. What the ...

NICOLE. Max?

MAX. We must have too many things going at the same time and blew a fuse. Wait a sec, I saw a flashlight by the fridge. *(Max stumbles up into the kitchen. Sound of him hitting furniture.)* Shit!

NICOLE. You OK?

MAX. Fine. Wait. Don't anybody move!

TROY. You need help?

MAX. No. Wait. Wait. Here. Owww.

NICOLE. Max! Are you OK? *(Max finds the flashlight and snaps it on.)*

MAX. I think I saw a fuse box downstairs. *(Max exits to the basement to fix the fuse.)*

TROY. How much are we paying for this dump anyway?

MAX. *(Off.)* DID THAT DO ANYTHING?

NICOLE. NO! WHERE ARE YOU?

MAX. *(Off.)* I DON'T THINK IT'S THE FUSE! *(Troy and Spoon are groping each other in the dark.)*

SPOON. Actually this isn't so bad. Take your time. *(Max enters, wiping cobwebs out of his hair.)*

MAX. I'm pretty sure it's not the fuse. They must have candles and matches somewhere. Hold this. *(Nicole holds the flashlight. Max rummages through drawers.)*

NICOLE. Let's call that Nat guy.

20

MAX. What's his number? Uh, Nicole, read the number off that note on the mantle. *(Nicole uses the flashlight to make her way to the fireplace. Max picks up the house phone.)*

SPOON. I'll find some candles.

MAX. On the fridge I think.

NICOLE. 2-5-5-7-3 ...

MAX. Wait. *(Spoon lights candles.)*

TROY. *(Singing:)* "Strangers in the night ... "

MAX. Shut up, Troy. Something's wrong with the phone.

NICOLE. What?

MAX. Fast busy signal.

SPOON. Probably everybody's using their phone. Overload.

NICOLE. You think?

MAX. Try your cell, Spoon.

NICOLE. I don't like this, Max! What if it's a terrorist attack or something?

TROY. Nicole, it's a fuse.

NICOLE. It's not a fuse. Max just checked the fuse.

TROY. Well, it's something. But it's not a terrorist attack. Terrorists don't attack renovated barns.

MAX. It's cool. It's cool.

SPOON. Oh, shit, my cell just went dead. Troy, where's the charger?

TROY. Where you going to plug it in?

SPOON. Oh. Right.

TROY. Here, I got mine. What's the number?

NICOLE. Well, it says 2-5-5-7-3-1 ... but you need the area code. What's the area code up here?

MAX. Uh ... shit. I have the real estate agent's number in my wallet.

NICOLE. Look on the phone. The phone, the house phone.

MAX. Oh, right. *(Max takes a candle and tries to inspect the phone.)* It's either 518 or 618, I can't make it out.

TROY. Max. Don't bother. My cell won't lock on. Just keeps searching. *(Headlights can be seen outside. A powerful light waves through the gloom in the mud room.)*

NICOLE. Oh wow. Max! This is freaky.

NAT. Hallo? *(Nat enters. His Coleman lamp illuminates the room.)*

MAX. Yes! Hi! Nat? Great!

NAT. Electric's out.

TROY. Is *that* why it's so dark in here!

MAX. At first I thought it was a breaker or a fuse ...

NICOLE. Is it something serious?

NAT. Nah. Probably some knucklehead hit a telephone pole. Take 'em couple of hours to fix it. Happens all the time. *(Nat has gone to the sink and begun to fill some pans and large bowls with water.)*

MAX. A telephone pole?

NAT. Sorry 'bout that. Just the way it is up here.

NICOLE. And they can fix it, what did you say, two hours?

NAT. Usually that's what it takes. Might take all night. Really dunno at this point. Look, you got candles and I'll leave this lamp here. The water pump runs on electric, this is just the water left in the pipes. Should hold you for the night. Just don't flush. And the oil burner needs a spark, so you might want to put some big logs in the fire before you go to bed. But hey, you're on vacation, right? Kick back, enjoy the quiet. I'll be by in the morning, check in on you. OK? Just watch out for the mountain lions. They're hungry this time of year. Just jokin.' *(Laughs.)* Alright then. Night all. *(Nat leaves.)*

TROY. Well there you go. The terrorists drove all the way up here and ran into a telephone pole.

SPOON. Leave it alone, Troy.

NICOLE. *(Pensive.)* So.

SPOON. So here we are. No lights. But that's not so bad.

TROY. And we can't flush.

SPOON. We *can*. We just, you know, shouldn't.

NICOLE. Max?

MAX. Here we are! It's like a camping trip.

TROY. Should we crack out the marshmallows and sing songs around the fire?

NICOLE. I'm going to bed. *(Nicole heads upstairs.)*

MAX. Nicole? Are you OK?

NICOLE. Yeah. Just … you know, tired.

MAX. OK. I'll be up in a sec.

TROY. You know what? I'm going to crash too.

MAX. Well, if everybody …

SPOON. Look how pretty the fire is.

MAX. Yeah. It is. It's primal isn't it? *(Troy makes his way upstairs.)*

TROY. G'night.

MAX. Night.

SPOON. The flames never stop changing. A million shapes and colors. And it's all the energy of the tree's life, all those years of living, just exploding outward into the air. Maybe that's what happens to us when we die. All our energy just flies out of us.

(Spoon has become transfixed by the fire. Max, not sure how to participate in Spoon's reverie, walks to a window and looks out.)
MAX. Dark out there. *(Spoon says nothing. Max moves as if to go to the stairs, then tries the phone one more time. Obviously, nothing. He hangs up. Blackout.)*

Scene 3

Morning. The fireplace is ablaze. Nicole is fussing around the kitchen, cleaning up nervously. Troy wanders up to her, reading from one of Max's books. Bread and coffee is laid out. The dirty dishes are there from the night before.

TROY. Did you know that Frederick Nietzsche died of tertiary syphilis? Spent the last ten years of his life totally paralyzed and nuts. Just like Voltaire. Just like Van Gogh. All the greats go mad.
NICOLE. Van Gogh. *(Pronounces it Van Goch.)*
TROY. What?
NICOLE. Van Gogh. The correct pronunciation is Van Gogh.
TROY. Van Gogh. Got it. Nicole. We should do a book together. I need to get close to your editing prowess.
NICOLE. A book?
TROY. A novel. I just finished it. I'll give you across-the-board participation — movie rights, TV, whatever you want.
NICOLE. *(Distracted.)* You wrote a novel?
TROY. I could have gone anywhere with it, but I wanted you to see it first. I have pages with me if you want to read them.
NICOLE. I don't think I can read anything right now.
TROY. Why not?
NICOLE. I have other things on my mind.
TROY. Like what?
NICOLE. Well, for one thing, I thought this "power outage" was going to last two hours. It's been over ten. The cell phones won't lock on. All the food in the fridge is about to spoil. I dunno.
TROY. Put it out on the porch.
NICOLE. You cannot put caviar out on the porch.
TROY. Then I'll eat it now. For brunch. *(Troy picks up the caviar*

and eats it out of the tin. Nicole watches him with curious disgust.)

NICOLE. Doesn't this bother you?

TROY. Yes. It's an indecent violation of excellent caviar. But I have no choice. By the way, you're going to love my book. Why don't I read you the first chapter? I'll go grab the pages. *(Troy goes to his bedroom as Max enters carrying a small sack of groceries. He throws car keys on the counter.)*

MAX. Well, that didn't work out so great.

NICOLE. What happened?

MAX. I guess you need electricity to make the gas pumps work. *So* the gas station's closed. And there's no milk, no bread, no newspapers. No cash machine.

NICOLE. Did you talk to anyone? *(Troy enters with his "pages," puts them down, continues eating caviar.)*

MAX. The guy at the store, "Slim," says it has nothing to do with a telephone pole. It's some kind of problem with "the grid." *(To Troy.)* You two were up pretty late.

TROY. Oh, you heard us? We didn't flush.

MAX. Uh … no. I mean … never mind.

TROY. Oh, right. Sorry about that, she gets kind of loud, what can I say? At least she doesn't *bark*. I had a girlfriend once who sounded like a …

NICOLE. Wait a minute, *guys!* Max! "Grid"? What does … what does that mean? "Grid"?

MAX. I have no idea.

NICOLE. Well, why didn't you ask your buddy "Slim"?

MAX. Nicole, please take that tone out of your voice. I'm not one of your minions.

NICOLE. Maybe we should just pack up and go back to the city?

MAX. No way! We'll just take a ride down to that big grocery store, stock up. Then we'll be set.

NICOLE. Were you able to use the pay phone? Call Sara? Tell her what's happening? Or my mother? I should call my mother.

MAX. Pay phones are out too. I tried to get some kind of news on the car radio, but all I got was static.

NICOLE. Static…?

MAX. There's only one station up here in the first place and they must need electricity too.

TROY. *(*Twilight Zone *theme:)* Doo-doo-doo-doo, doo-doo-doo-doo.

MAX. Troy, *please! (Noticing.)* What's that? The caviar?

24

TROY. Yes. It is. Want some? It's very good.

NICOLE. Max. What do you think?

MAX. I think we paid for the place. We're here now. Let's give it a chance.

NICOLE. But do you think it could be something like, you know, something someone *did?* On purpose? *(Troy pours himself a Stoli.)*

TROY. Ever see that Henry Fonda movie *Fail-Safe?* He's talking on the phone to the prime minister of Russia and the atom bombs start dropping and then there's this sound, like "BOOOOOOOOO," and someone says, "What's that sound?" And someone else says, "That's the sound of the phones melting in the fireball on the other end of the line."

MAX. Troy, that's not funny, OK? And it has nothing to do with what we're talking about.

TROY. Have a drink, Max. You're on vacation.

MAX. I don't drink in the morning. *(To Nicole:)* Nicole, what are you saying?

NICOLE. Bet they have electricity in Saint Bart's.

MAX. That's not fair. You wanted to come up here as much as I did. In fact, it was *your* idea to go on this vacation.

NICOLE. There are a thousand places we could have gone.

MAX. And any one of them could have a blackout just like this. Jesus, Nicole! *(Spoon enters through the mud room carrying a coal scuttle full of pine cones. Spoon slips an arm around Troy and they kiss.)*

SPOON. Good morning! *(Indicating the coal scuttle.)* Check out what I've been collecting. They're all over the ground out there. *Millions.*

NICOLE. Those are called "pine cones." They fall off the pine trees.

SPOON. Uh, I *know* that. Duh.

MAX. I thought you were still in bed?

SPOON. On a day like this? I've been up since six. Look, they're so beautiful! Like little sculptures.

TROY. You hungry, baby? We have caviar.

SPOON. You guys have to get *outside.* The air is practically shimmering with sunshine. Everything is so alive! I saw a red fox and a bald eagle, I think it was a bald eagle, down by the pond. And the pond, it's like molten crystal. Everything is so still and perfect.

NICOLE. It's getting colder. We should stoke up the fireplace.

MAX. Got it. *(Troy pulls a joint from his suit-jacket pocket. Lights it.)*

TROY. Stoke up! Excellent idea.

MAX. Troy, it's eleven o'clock in the morning!

TROY. I know, it's getting late. *(Spoon takes the joint and toasts.)*

SPOON. To nature, to serenity, to really getting away from it all. To pine cones.

MAX. I thought you didn't drink?

SPOON. Pot's herbal. Medicinal.

MAX. *(Glum.)* True. I forgot about that part.

NICOLE. Max, the people at the store, did they look worried?

MAX. Well, they weren't very talkative, but no, they didn't look particulary concerned. *(The joint gets passed to Nicole, who takes it absent mindedly.)*

NICOLE. *(Toking.)* Yeah?

SPOON. Maybe there's a computer malfunction somewhere? All the electricity is routed by computer systems that regulate the flow of electricity through the grid.

MAX. The *grid!* You know what a grid is?

SPOON. Everyone from California knows what a grid is. It's you know, where the electricity comes from.

NICOLE. OK, but Spoon, if this is because of some kind of problem with the "grid," then what does that have to do with the phones?

TROY. Phones need electricity don't they? Right? I mean, how *do* phones work, anyway? "Mr. Watson, come here I need you." That's as far as I got. *(Spoon touches Troy as she takes the joint from him.)*

SPOON. Phones are pretty simple. *(Takes a hit.)* Sound waves cause the "diaphram" to vibrate and the vibrations disturb a magnetic field which in turn induces an electrical current. *That's* transmitted to *another* phone causing the diaphram in *it* to vibrate. *(Exhales a cloud of smoke.)* Reproducing the original sound. See?

TROY. Isn't she great? *(They kiss.)*

MAX. It *is* amazing when you think about it. Some unseen turbine hundreds of miles away fabricates all this energy which courses over a vast, interlocking system of millions of fragile wires, continuously, silently, like an enormous river of electrons pulsing through a vast nerve network towards its destination where it becomes power again, making the ... the tiny blades of the coffee grinder spin.

TROY. *(Mocking:)* Yeah, wow man.

MAX. Shuttup. I'm trying to be serious. Where does electricity come from anyway? Like where *is* the generator? I don't know. Do you? And what kind of generator is it? Nuclear? Coal? Do they use coal? Windmills? *(Stoned:)* Maybe they just have this massive rubber band and they wind it up really, really tight ...

SPOON. You know what it could be? *(Takes a huge hit.)*

MAX. Tell us!

SPOON. A *storm!* Last year an enormous storm in the Midwest knocked out electricity, water and phones in four states.

MAX. But there's been no snow for weeks.

TROY. *Far away,* dude. Far, far away.

SPOON. Yeah, far, far, far away.

TROY. The old flapping butterfly wing in China routine.

MAX. The *what?*

TROY. You know, the butterfly wing flaps in China, makes a miniscule puff, which gets amplified until it's a flurry, then a breeze, one thing leads to the next and by the time it gets here it's this enormo destructo tornado. *(Beat.)*

SPOON. It could be a million things. We live in a highly vulnerable social structure. One thing impacts on the next in a million ways. The currency exchange shifts, some country in Asia defaults on its loans, which affects a highly leveraged energy corporation like Enron, bing-bang, your lights go out.

MAX. How come when *I* smoke pot my IQ goes *down* and Spoon's goes *up?*

SPOON. *(Into it:)* It could be something systemic affecting the population! Remember that movie with Dustin Hoffman and everyone had to wear spacesuits to prevent contamination from some insane virus?

TROY. *Outbreak.* Warner's. 1995. CAA package.

SPOON. Yeah. *Outbreak*, that was pretty crazy. That was sort of like this. Small town. No one knows what's going on.

MAX. But that was totally fictional!

SPOON. Well what about anthrax? That's real. Terrorists are real. In 1984 the Soviet Union launched a smallpox outbreak that killed thousands of people in the middle of Sibera. *(Nicole has been following intently.)*

NICOLE. That's right! There are scientists in Iran at this very moment, trying to create biowarfare cruise missiles. We did that book three years ago, the scariest thing I ever read. And what about ebola, Max? That's the most contagious thing in the world. Zero survival rate.

MAX. Wait a minute, how do we get to biowarfare from a power blackout?

TROY. Wouldn't that be a trip? The plague rampaging through the streets, causing havoc and chaos! Looting! Martial law!

MAX. This is absurd!

NICOLE. Wasn't it 1918 or 1919 when the flu killed all those people? Like twenty million, was it twenty million? *(Stoned.)* Twenty *million?*

TROY. Twenty million, that sounds about right.

NICOLE. Or was it thirty?

SPOON. It *was* thirty. Definitely thirty. *(Beat.)* Wow. That would so screw things up. *(Beat.)*

NICOLE. It's so quiet all of a sudden. *(Overwhelming silence.)* I want to call my mother.

MAX. Nicole … *(Nicole stands, panicky.)*

NICOLE. Shit. I can't tell whether I'm stoned or if I'm having an anxiety attack.

TROY. I have Prozac if you want it.

MAX. You're on Prozac?

TROY. No, I just have it. You know, in case I want to see things from a different perspective.

SPOON. I saw this movie where this terrorist brought a small nuclear device into the city in a *rowboat.* That could happen *so* easily. Probably just a matter of time.

NICOLE. Stop for a sec, Spoon, please?

MAX. Nicole, you OK?

NICOLE. I just need some fresh air. *(Nicole gets up to go out but doesn't leave.)*

NAT. *(Off.)* Hallo!

MAX. Oh Jeez, it's Nat. Troy, throw the joint in the fireplace.

NICOLE. Oh, I can't deal with this guy right now! *(Nat enters carrying jugs of water.)*

NAT. How we all doin'? We hanging in there?

MAX. Oh, hey, Nat, hey, come on in.

TROY. *(Jovial.)* Hey Nat! How's the sheep farm?

NAT. Sheep?! No sheep around this way. You guys getting by without the cable TV?

MAX. Pretty well. You?

NAT. Oh, I dunno. We lose the juice up here so often, it doesn't really affect us. *(Beat.)* I brought you some water and candles. Should hold you a couple of days.

NICOLE. Couple of days?!

NAT. From what I've heard, there's been a big storm about two hundred miles north of here …

TROY. Flap, flap.

MAX. *(Ignoring Troy.)* Yeah?

NAT. And a big transformer or something blew out. That's what the state troopers are telling everybody. Probably take a couple of days to fix.

MAX. A storm. Really? *(To Nat.)* A transformer? Hmmm.

NAT. That's what they say. Why, you hear something different?

NICOLE. We thought it could be, you know, something serious.

NAT. Like what?

TROY. The end of the world, something along those lines.

NAT. Nope. Sorry. I didn't hear anything like that.

MAX. How many towns are affected?

NAT. Pretty much all the towns.

NICOLE. What's "all the towns"?

NAT. All the towns in the county. Next county too, so they say.

NICOLE. So what's going to happen? I mean what are people doing about it?

NAT. Ah, people lived up here for hundreds of years without electricity. We can get by for a few days. You got food and somebody to keep you warm, what else do you need? What *is* that smell?

TROY. Weed. You want some?

NAT. Weed? *(Beat.)* Sure, why not? *(Troy resusitates the joint. Lights it. They pass the joint.)*

TROY. Check this shit out. This is the shit Kevin Spacey smoked in *American Beauty.*

NICOLE. A few days. That's not so good. Max?

MAX. You hear anything on the radio, Nat?

NAT. Radio? Radio's out, no electricity.

NICOLE. "Radio's out." Great.

TROY. So Nat, what do you do up here for fun? You hunt?

NAT. Not really, no time. In fact, I gotta get up some fencing before the first snow, or the deer'll eat all the shrubs right down. They love those rhodie buds, munch on 'em like candy.

TROY. Yeah. They do. *(Pause.)* What's a "rhodie bud"?

NAT. You know, flowers. Have to do the gutters too. I'll wait 'til you guys leave.

MAX. Gutters?

NAT. Well, this time of year, the roof gutters get all filled up with pine needles, then snow piles up on 'em, next thing you know, you got the ice creepin' up under your shingles and a leaky roof. Every year I get the calls, "Nat, help! I got a leaky roof." And I wanna say, "Why don't you cut down that friggin' pine tree you got hanging over your gutters!" you know? Pardon my French. *(Laughs.)* People don't think. They plant the trees right up next to the house, roots clog the plumbing, squirrels get in the attic. If I had my way, I'd get out the chain saw cut 'em all down. Toss 'em in the chipper. *(Taking a hit.)* This stuff's almost as good as Zeke's. *(Nat gets more animated and relaxed. The group is transfixed.)*

MAX. "Zeke"?

NAT. Has about an acre of pot behind his chicken sheds. Chicken poop is one hell of a fertilizer.

TROY. Yup. I've always found that to be true.

SPOON. Don't the police do anything?

NAT. Only police around here are staties and they stick to the thruway.

NICOLE. Oh.

NAT. It's pretty much live and let live up here. Lots of people who like their privacy: hippies, hillbillies.

NICOLE. Hillbillies?

NAT. Oh, yeah, you know, with the overalls and the long beards? Make pies out of woodchucks. You mind if I...? *(Indicates fruit bowl.)*

NICOLE. No, no. Go ahead. These hillbillies, how close are they? *(Nat takes an apple and kicks back.)*

NAT. Five miles? Two miles? Couldn't say, they're up there in the woods. They're like the bikers. They keep to themselves.

TROY. Bikers?

NAT. *(Laughing.)* Oh sure. They're a riot. There's this one big dude, Mal? Has a swastika tattooed right in the middle of his forehead.

MAX. This is a buddy of yours?

NAT. Hell *no!* In fact, two years ago he was beating on his girlfriend at the Volunteer Fireman's Fourth of July barbecue and I grabbed him, right? He took a bite right out of my side.

SPOON. He bit you? With his teeth? That must have hurt.

NAT. It's OK, I just chucked his head right into the cinderblock wall, knocked him out cold. *(Smiling.)* We all ended up going to the hospital together. *(Nicole has retreated to a corner and has grown quiet.)*

SPOON. Wow.

TROY. Nothing like a fireman's barbecue for a good time.

NAT. That's true. *(Noticing Nicole.)* Are you okay?

NICOLE. Me? Oh, I'm fine ...

MAX. Thanks for the water, Nat.

NAT. Sure. Sure. *(Beat.)* Well, I better get going. Mom's waiting lunch for me. *(Nat gets up. As he passes Nicole:)* Bye.

NICOLE. Bye. And thanks. Nat.

NAT. No problem. *(Nat's gone.)*

MAX. Nicole? You alright? *(Nicole finds and starts flipping through a yellow pages.)*

SPOON. See, it's no biggie. So why don't we all get some fresh air and chill?

TROY. Yeah, let's go see that molten crystal pond. Max? *(Troy and Spoon begin to move to the door. Nicole finds what she needs, picks up the phone.)*

NICOLE. *Yes!* Dial tone. See? Positive thinking. *(Dials, listens.)*

MAX. Phone's working?

NICOLE. "All circuits are busy." Fuck! *(Nicole pushes more buttons.)* Maybe it's only long distance that's screwed up.

MAX. Who could you possibly be calling?

NICOLE. *(Into phone.)* Yeah, hi, could I? OK. *(To Max.)* Now I'm on hold.

MAX. Who are you calling, Nicole?

NICOLE. *(Into phone.)* Is this the Marriott? Yeah, hi, I want to make a reservation for ... *(Listening.)* I know, I know, we're about twenty miles from you, we have the same problem that's why ... Uh, OK. *(To Max:)* I'm not just going to sit here, Max.

MAX. Nicole.

SPOON. I hate those big hotel chains.

TROY. Sweetness, there are no Four Seasons this far from civilization. *(To Nicole.)* Make sure they have goose-down pillows.

NICOLE. I'm holding. Yes, I understand but ... excuse me, may I finish? I am a platinum card holder and I ... I know that, I understand that, you have no rooms for tonight, but what I'm saying is, yes ... My company spends a lot of money on lodging and I'm just saying, I need a *room* tonight, two rooms actually and I would appreciate ... Yes, I'll hold.

MAX. Nicole, we don't need a room. And besides she's not going to help you out.

NICOLE. *(To Max:)* YES SHE *IS!!!* If she doesn't have a room, she has to tell me where I can find one. That's part of the "platinum executive program." *(To phone:)* ... Hello? Hello? Yes? I know that, I understand that, that has been explained to me *twice* now. But ...

MAX. We have a perfectly good place right here.

NICOLE. *(Gritted teeth, to Max:)* MAX! *(To phone:)* What? No, I wasn't speaking to you. But *no,* don't put me on hold. Well, you

31

asked me and I'm saying don't. *(Listens, then suddenly subdued.)* What? But, how can you…? Oh, then … thank you. *(Nicole gently hangs the phone up. Max picks it up.)*

MAX. Line's dead. No dial tone at all now. *(In a funk, Nicole walks over and slumps onto the couch.)*

NICOLE. We can't get a room because they're going to close the hotel tomorrow.

MAX. Close the hotel? How can they do that?

NICOLE. The whole region is without electricity. Some vacation.

TROY. I've got the munchies and I'm making lunch, who's hungry?

NICOLE. Those dishes aren't clean.

TROY. Clean enough. How about crabmeat salad everyone? Use up the mayo. In another six hours it won't be mayo anymore, it will be deadly poison. *(No response.)* I take that as a yes.

SPOON. C'mon, it's really beautiful outside, let's go for that walk, then have lunch? *(No one responds. Troy continues to bustle about.)*

TROY. *(Singing.)* "The end of the world as we know it."

NICOLE. Troy, please wash those dishes before using them.

SPOON. It's so nice out! *(Nicole crowds Troy, who is now opening the cans of crabmeat with a can opener.)*

NICOLE. Are you washing those or just rinsing?

TROY. Nicole, relax.

NICOLE. I'm just saying that if you're cleaning, it's usually a wise idea to use some kind of dishwashing detergent.

TROY. Oh, is it? I didn't know that. Any particular brand?

NICOLE. Just, just … you know what? Just leave all that and I'll do it later.

TROY. No, really I'm curious. Why is this so important to you?

NICOLE. To kill the germs!

TROY. What germs?

SPOON. *(Trying not to be amused.)* Troy, stop it!

MAX. Nicole, let's all go for a walk?

TROY. What germs? Where?

NICOLE. Germs. Germs! *Germs,* you know? Louis Pasteur? Modern science? Sanitation?

TROY. This is very bourgeois of you, Nicole. *(Nicole jumps up, pushes Troy away from the sink.)* Well, excuse me! *(Nicole takes the dishes Troy just "washed" and puts them back in the sink. Begins cleaning frenetically.)*

MAX. Lemme help with that.

NICOLE. No! I'm fine. Really. *(Nicole grabs for the crabmeat can, misjudges the distance and puts her hand onto the lid and cuts her hand. Blood drips onto the counter.)*

NICOLE. Ow!!! SHIT!

TROY. Did you cut yourself?

NICOLE. Yes, you asshole!

TROY. Oh, is that blood?

NICOLE. Get away from me! *(Nicole whirls away from Troy, now spilling the crabmeat salad all over the floor.)* Shit!

TROY. My salad! *(Nicole wraps her hand, there's blood staining the white towel.)*

MAX. Nicole, that doesn't look so good. *(Max runs to the bathroom.)*

SPOON. Nicole, let me see it.

NICOLE. *(Maddened.)* NO!!! Everyone go away!

TROY. That's a lot of blood. *(Max flies back down the stairs.)*

MAX. All they've got are these bandaids and Neosporin. Let me see it Nicole.

TROY. Do you want me to finish doing the dishes?

MAX. TROY, WILL YOU SHUT THE FUCK UP! *(Nicole curls over, weeping softly.)* Honey, it'll be alright. Come on, there must be a hospital around here somewhere. We'll have a doctor look at it.

NICOLE. What hospital? Where?

MAX. I don't know, we'll ask them at Slim's.

SPOON. Maybe we should call Nat.

MAX. Right. *(Max picks up the house phone. Listens.)* Still nothing. *(Max picks up Troy's cell. Punches numbers, listens.)* Dammit! *(Max throws the phone, shattering it.)*

TROY. That thing was state-of-the-art.

MAX. That's not what's important at the moment, is it, Troy?

TROY. Well, uh, yeah, it is. What do we do without a phone?

MAX. Nicole's cell.

NICOLE.   SPOON.

My battery's dead.   Mine too.

MAX. LOOK, I DON'T KNOW! Let's deal with one thing at a time. Come on, Nicole, let's just go.

NICOLE. What if we run out of gas? You said there's no gas stations.

MAX. We have enough gas to find a hospital.

NICOLE. What if we get lost? Or get a flat tire? Or they can't see me right away and we get stuck driving back in the dark and a bunch of bikers find us? Or hillbillies?

MAX. That's not going to happen.

NICOLE. I think it's stopped bleeding.

MAX. Are you sure?

NICOLE. I don't want to go driving around right now, OK?

SPOON. I don't know about you, but I'm still a little high. I don't really want to go where there are, you know, people.

MAX. Should we wait for a while?

SPOON. Wait, see how it's feeling.

MAX. Yeah. That's a plan. If it starts to feel worse.

TROY. Remember that movie *Deliverance*? *(Mimics the banjo picking.)*

SPOON. Troy, come outside with me.

TROY. What? *(Troy and Spoon leave as Max stands over Nicole, protective.)*

MAX. OK.

NICOLE. OK. *(Long beat.)* Max, I want to go.

MAX. To the hospital?

NICOLE. No. I want to go home. I want to leave.

MAX. That doesn't really make sense, Nicole. I mean, A) I'm not sure we can find gas. B) Do you really want to drive for hours and maybe run the risk of getting stuck somewhere? Hotels are closing. There's no electricity for miles around. I mean, we're here. What's the big deal?

NICOLE. Two days?

MAX. What if I told you that you only had to endure this for another twelve hours? Would you do it?

NICOLE. Max, that's not the point.

MAX. Twenty-four hours? Thirty-six hours? I mean, we've gone on camping trips that were much more difficult than this. Everyone's just getting very wound up.

NICOLE. Don't tell me I'm wound up.

MAX. Look, this isn't pleasant. But it's not the end of the world.

NICOLE. How do you know?

MAX. Nicole. You heard Nat, it's a broken transformer.

NICOLE. That's what someone said.

MAX. Tomorrow, maybe the day after, we'll know more. And when we do, we can decide then. Right now, our best bet is to throw some logs on the fire and kick back. Right? It'll be good to live without a phone for a couple of days. We've never done this. Really spent time together like this. It's not a big deal. They'll fix it.

NICOLE. Yeah.

MAX. Remember, the things you worry about the most, never happen.

NICOLE. I wasn't worrying about this. *(Nicole looks at her hand, stands and goes to the bathroom. Max unsure of what he should do, checks the fireplace, finds that they are out of wood, walks up to the mud room. We see him find an axe there, which he picks up and goes outside. We hear the sound of wood splitting as the lights go down.)*

End Act One

ACT TWO

Scene 1

One week later, daylight. From offstage comes the sound of an axe splitting wood mingled with dogs barking. Stacks of empty egg trays and plastic water jugs. Guttered candles have dripped wax over every surface. The stone face of the fireplace is stained with soot. Pine cones and pine boughs decorate every edge and surface of the room. Spoon sits at the table wearing a fuzzy overcoat, drinking glasses of something she pours from an unlabeled plastic jug. The sound of chopping stops. Max, wearing an old parka and sporting a week's worth of beard stubble, enters hauling an armload of wood. Throws it by the fireplace.

MAX. Fucking dogs out there. Hanging around.

SPOON. I think they're abandoned. I gave them some eggs to eat.

MAX. Great. Tomorrow there'll be twice as many.

SPOON. Have some of Nat's cider. It's good. He calls it "applejack." *(Max rummages for food in the kitchen.)*

MAX. Where's the homemade peanut butter?

SPOON. Troy finished it two days ago. *(Nicole comes out of a bedroom and groggily heads for a bathroom. Her hand is bandaged.)*

MAX. Fuck! I can't eat another egg. *(To Nicole:)* It's one o'clock in the afternoon, Nicole. *(Nicole doesn't reply. Slams the door. To Spoon:)* She stays up all night and sleeps all day.

SPOON. You know, it's funny, I *like* eggs. I think we're lucky to have 'em, you know? And the stove works, so that's a good thing. I mean, this isn't that bad. Is it? The weather's nice and clear and crispy. We're surrounded by nature and woods and all that stuff. And there's no phones. No agents or publicists calling up all day long. Can't go shopping. Can't do anything but just, you know, be calm. I like this. I like this a lot. I don't think I've felt this clear in a long long time. You know? I get up early. I do my yoga. I go for walks. I breathe fresh air all day. I watch the clouds in the sky. I can

36

think. And when it gets dark I go to bed. It's like a dream come true. Back in L.A., all I do is get stuck in traffic and talk on my cel phone and use my credit card and worry about my career. I needed this. I really, really needed this. *(Nicole emerges from the bathroom. Goes to the kitchen, gets a kettle, fills it from a jug of water, puts it on the stove. She favors her good hand. Max watches Nicole; she ignores him.)*

MAX. I could use some help you know.

NICOLE. Max, please don't start. I just woke up.

SPOON. Good morning Nicole. I mean, good afternoon.

MAX. If you went to bed on time ...

NICOLE. How am I supposed to help you when I have this? *(She holds up her hand.)*

MAX. We should have had those stitches out two days ago.

NICOLE. I'm not going back there, Max. Can you imagine what that place is like now? Like something you see on the evening news! All those pathetic people lined up. Babies crying. And what do you think that hospital smells like now, a week later? I don't want some local yokel country doctor who's had two hours of sleep screwing around with my hand. I need my hand, it's useful. OK? I'll deal with the stitches when we get home.

MAX. Does it still hurt?

NICOLE. *I don't want to talk about it right now,* OK? Can I have five minutes to myself before you start nagging me?

MAX. *(Resigned.)* I'm not nagging you.

NICOLE. Just go do your frontiersman bit and chop your wood. Go swing your big axe. *(Spoon snickers. Max gives her a hateful look. Troy rushes in. He's carrying bags of groceries, throws them down.)*

TROY. I just got stopped at a *checkpoint.*

MAX. Checkpoint? What do you mean "checkpoint"?

TROY. So I stop. And this one redneck comes over and says, "Sir, please step out of your vehicle and stand to one side."

SPOON. He was a cop?

TROY. I don't know. They had *guns,* Spoon! What was I going to do? Run over them? Give 'em an excuse to fine-tune the crosshairs on their rifles' scopes?

MAX. That's nuts.

TROY. So I get out of the car while this jerk checks my license and registration. Then another one with a crewcut and an army jacket, you know, Special Forces wannabe, sidles up and wants to know what I'm *doing* around here. How come I'm so far from California? I tell him I'm on vacation. That gets him even more wound up.

Wants to know how much I'm renting the place for, who else is up here with me? I told him it was none of his fucking business.

MAX.   NICOLE.

Oh jeez!   Troy!

TROY. Oh yeah. Guy gives me this long look like he's going to *do* something. What's he going to *do?* Arrest me? Beat me up?

MAX. You shouldn't push it, Troy.

TROY. Ah, fuck him. Fuck all of 'em. Did your buddy Nat stop by today?

MAX. He's not my buddy.

TROY. Sure he is. Mister Authenticity. Laughing at us behind our backs.

MAX. The guy has been very helpful.

TROY. The guy is having the time of his life. *(Troy starts unpacking all kinds of groceries from the paper bags.)* I can see him hanging out with all his pals. Laughing about the fools from the city stuck up at the Murphy place, freezing their nuts off, chewing on pine cones.

MAX. That's the way you see it. That's just your prejudice against him.

TROY. Yeah? Before I got stopped? There was this bonfire down by a Little League field. So I figure I'll go down and see if anyone had any news. And by the fire all these local guys are hunched over this, I don't know what it was, maybe a cow carcass, maybe a moose, I don't know, sawing at it with knives. Chopping off the legs, the neck. Not talking, just kind of hacking and grunting. Blood smeared all over their pants, their jackets. I could smell the steaming guts spilled all over the dirt. One of 'em was working on the throat, totally focused, the sweat dripping off his nose, a cigarette hanging from his lips. His hands covered in gore. I must have been staring at him. He looked up at me and I realized. This guy hates me. He doesn't know me, but he hates me, because he knows I don't belong here. I left. Just got in the car and left.

MAX. This is you, Troy. This is you projecting all of this on these people. On Nat. Nat hasn't done a thing to you.

TROY. Yet. *(Nicole has focused on the things Troy has been unpacking.)*

NICOLE. What's all this?

TROY. Hey, I don't know about you, but I need my coffee in the morning. So I went and got some. *(To Nicole.)* Plus I found frozen steaks. Chocolate-covered potato chips. You'd be amazed what's out there.

MAX. "Found"?

TROY. Look around you. There are empty summer homes all over the place up here. Those people don't need this stuff. *We* do. *(Troy focuses on Spoon for the first time.)* Whatcha drinking there, Spoon?

SPOON. This is cider.

TROY. *Hard* cider, my dear. As in "alcoholic beverage."

SPOON. Don't patronize me, Troy. OK?

TROY. I never patronize you, Spoon.

SPOON. Leave me alone. If I want to drink hard cider, I'll drink it. I really resent you mocking me in front of everybody. Treating me like some kind of bimbo.

TROY. Stop acting like a bimbo and I'll stop treating you like one.

SPOON. How do I act like a bimbo? Tell me! *How?*

TROY. The whole sunny, positive bit. Always smiling like you don't have a thought in your head. It's getting old. It's getting really, really boring.

SPOON. At least I don't bitch and moan all day like you. *That's* what's boring. *You're* the one who's boring. Is it my fault that I'm not suffering like you are?

TROY. Yes. It is. Because you're too dim-witted to notice how fucked-up this all is. And that's depressing.

MAX. Troy, take a Prozac.

TROY. I don't need a Prozac. *(Continuing his rant:)* Sitting on your ass, meditating, doing yoga. I'm out there finding food. Finding gas. What are you doing? Nothing. You think this is fun! This is your idea of a good time. Fresh air! Pine cones! Baby rabbits! I hate this. I HATE IT!

SPOON. Troy, don't yell at me.

TROY. I'm not yelling at you.

SPOON. My father used to yell at me. I will not be yelled at.

TROY. Please don't start sharing about your traumatic childhood. *(Spoon is on the verge of tears.)* And don't start crying, it's repulsive.

SPOON. No one's crying! *You're* the one who wanted to come on this, this whatever it is, "vacation." This was *your* agenda! And you didn't get what you wanted, so now you've turned into an total asshole.

MAX. Let's all calm down.

TROY. Spoon, just shuttup and drink your cider.

SPOON. Hey Max, you know why your best friend came on this vacation? To hang with his homies? He wants to sell his new novel to Nicole.

TROY. You're right, Spoon. You shouldn't drink, you become

delusional.

SPOON. Did you tell Max about your novel?

MAX. You have a novel, Troy? *(To Nicole.)* Did Troy tell you about a novel?

TROY. I just wanted Nicole to give me some input. I wasn't ready to ... uh ...

MAX. Oh. Well, I'll read it. Whenever. *(Beat.)* I was wondering why you came. I thought, I have so few real friends in the world. I can depend on Troy. He seems like a jerk, but he's real. He's my "best friend."

TROY. I *am* your friend. To the degree that anyone is a friend to anyone.

MAX. We need more wood. *(Max heads for the door.)*

TROY. You may be smarter than me, Max, but I'm the one who gets it done. I get it done, Max, because I'm not afraid to make a move. *(Max goes out and we hear him chopping. Nicole picks up her tea and goes back to the bedroom. Troy speaks to her back.)* Nicole, I only wanted you to see it first. *(Nicole closes the door. Beat.)* Thanks, Spoon.

SPOON. I'm sorry. *(Troy picks up the TV. He unplugs it and carries it to the kitchen. Then starts to pack odd items in a box. Watching him:)* What are you doing?

TROY. We should have left a week ago.

SPOON. Where are you taking the TV?

TROY. It's called barter.

SPOON. But there's no gas.

TROY. There's gas.

SPOON. One gallon at a time. Where are we going to go on one gallon?

TROY. To the next gas station.

SPOON. Troy, you don't even know if there *is* another gas station.

TROY. Of course there's another gas station! Do you think it's like this a hundred miles from here? This is just some fucked-up place.

SPOON. *(Puts her face in her hands.)* But we don't ... you don't even know if the roads are open. *(Troy relents, touches her shoulder.)*

TROY. Hey ... *(To himself:)* What am I doing here? My hands are covered with blisters from chopping. My shoes, my beautiful shoes, are encrusted with mud and deer shit. These shoes cost three hundred and fifty dollars, look at them.

SPOON. They're just shoes.

TROY. No. They're *me*. I'm letting myself go. I stink. I'm hungry

40

and tired all the time. So cold I can't think straight. I have to get out of here.

SPOON. In a few days …

TROY. No. Not in a few days. Right now. I'm leaving.

SPOON. Troy. Whatever this is, we can get through it together.

TROY. No. *You* get through it. I shouldn't even be here. I should be in L.A. Right now. Right this minute, I should be sitting in a warm, spotless restaurant. Scrubbed floor, clean hands. Sipping bottled water, perusing a menu, a waiter at my side, eagerly awaiting my decision. *(Troy addresses the invisible waiter:)* Yes, I'd like to start with the tapenade, and follow that with the mesclun salad lightly sprinkled with a dressing of grapeseed oil and rare balsamic vinegars. Oh, warm sourdough breadsticks! Awesome. And yes, I'll have the grilled Chilean sea bass on the bed of marinated artichokes and roasted portobello mushrooms. What's that? I think you're right, Rothschild '87. Excellent choice. *(Spoon embraces Troy from behind.)*

SPOON. Baby, let's go to bed. You'll feel better.

TROY. No I won't.

SPOON. You will.

TROY. I don't want to.

SPOON. Because you think I'm repulsive? *(Troy breaks away and continues packing up the things he's taking.)*

TROY. People get what they deserve. I'm not waiting around for the other shoe to drop. *(Troy starts to walk out with the boxes.)*

SPOON. I want to come with you.

TROY. I'll be back after I gas up.

SPOON. Promise?

TROY. Hey … *(Troy kisses her quickly and leaves. Spoon pours a large glass of cider, finds a forgotten bottle of vodka, pours a shot into the glass, and knocks it back. She lights a cigarette. Gets up and walks to the upstage windows, watches Max chopping, returns to the table just as he enters with wood. Max enters with wood, goes to the fire and stokes it up. Spoon walks over to where Max is fooling with the fire.)*

SPOON. You make such a pretty fire, Max.

MAX. Thanks. *(Spoon touches Max's shoulder.)*

SPOON. You want a drink?

MAX. Not right now.

SPOON. It'll make you feel better.

MAX. What's the saying, "This too shall pass"?

SPOON. I love that saying.

MAX. *(Beat.)* Yeah. Well, this'll be over soon. *(Looking:)* Where's

41

the TV?

SPOON. Max. Could you do me a favor?

MAX. Sure.

SPOON. Could you give me a hug?

MAX. A hug?

SPOON. Just hold me. For a sec. Please?

MAX. Sure. *(Max stands and faces Spoon. Hugs her. The hug lasts a little too long.)*

SPOON. You're such a sweet guy, Max. You know that? I like you. I like you a lot.

MAX. I like you too. *(Max pulls himself from Spoon's embrace.)* Watch out, I might think you're trying to seduce me. *(Spoon says nothing because that is what she's doing. Uncomfortable pause as they both realize that. Nicole emerges from the bedrooms, grabs some hot water from the kettle and returns to her room.)* Troy wrote a book?

SPOON. Uh-huh.

MAX. What's it about?

SPOON. It's autobiographical. All about his crazy family and his crazy childhood.

MAX. I didn't know Troy had a crazy childhood.

SPOON. He was very poor. Brought up in foster homes.

MAX. Since when? I went to college with the guy, believe me, I know.

SPOON. Maybe he just never told you. *(Spoon finds her jacket and slips it on. Heads for the door.)*

MAX. Yeah. Maybe he didn't. Where are you going?

SPOON. Nowhere. Just for a walk.

MAX. Well, don't go too far. It's getting late. *(Spoon is almost out the door.)*

MAX. Where is Troy anyway?

SPOON. Out driving, I guess.

MAX. Do you know when he's coming back?

SPOON. No. *(Noticing.)* Hey, it's starting to snow. That's cool. I love snow. *(Spoon goes out. Long beat. Max goes to the door.)*

MAX. Spoon? SPOON? Wait a second. *(Max grabs his coat and leaves. Lights dim.)*

Scene 2

It's much darker now. Candles and the fireplace illuminate the space. Nicole sits at the large oak table; before her is an egg, which she spins with her good hand. She's drinking the hard cider. Max enters the kitchen, tosses his car keys on the counter.

MAX. Can't find her. Looked everywhere. Did Troy come back?
NICOLE. Troy's not coming back, Max. Isn't that obvious?
MAX. No. Nothing's obvious.
NICOLE. *(Flat.)* When I get home, I'm taking a long, hot bath. In fact I don't think I'll ever get out. *(Beat.)* I wonder if Billy ever made the deadline? *(Beat. Sound of gun being fired off.)*
MAX. What's that?
NICOLE. *(Flat.)* Hunters I guess. Getting closer. *(Another gunshot. Max plays with the fire in the fireplace, throws in a log. Nicole stands for the first time. She's not steady on her feet. She picks up her egg and wanders over to Max.)*
NICOLE. I love eggs. I wish we had *more* eggs.
MAX. *(Offhand.)* I don't. *(Nicole holds her egg up for inspection.)*
NICOLE. You know what I love about eggs?
MAX. What? *(Nicole tosses the egg in the air, catches it, tosses it, catches it.)*
NICOLE. They're so perfect. Perfect ... but ... *(Nicole lets the egg drop onto the floor, breaking.)*
MAX. Oh, shit. *(Nicole takes another egg from the box. Tosses it up and down.)*
NICOLE. Did you know, you can put a hundred pounds of pressure on an egg like this ... *(She pinches the egg from top and bottom.)* ... and it won't break? Won't. Very strong. A marvel of physics and construction.
MAX. Nicole.
NICOLE. An egg can take a huge, an incredible amount of pressure. I think I heard somewhere that if you place an egg the right way, you can run over it with a steamroller and it won't break. Or was it hit it with a sledgehammer? No that can't be it.
MAX. I never heard that. Have you been drinking?

NICOLE. No, I haven't been drinking! Wait, I got it wrong. An *elephant,* something with an elephant. An elephant can step on an egg and it won't crack. Isn't that amazing? That an egg could withstand that kind of pressure?

MAX. Nicole.

NICOLE. It is amazing. *But,* if you drop it: *(She lets go of the egg.)* The egg gets all fucked up. *(Max grabs some paper towels and starts mopping up the mess.)*

MAX. Please. *(Nicole drops another egg next to Max, now that he's cleaned up the first two.)*

NICOLE. So fragile. *(Nicole drops another egg. Max grabs her wrists.)*

MAX. Nicole. Nicole. Stop! *(Nicole won't meet Max's eyes.)*

NICOLE. Humpty Dumpty sat on a wall ... *(Max holds on to her wrists.)*

MAX. NICOLE!

NICOLE. Let go!

MAX. Stop it. You're scaring me. *(Nicole tears her wrists from Max and walks away.)*

NICOLE. Scaring *you?* You're out there somewhere, who knows if you're ever coming back or what! I'm here all alone. Someone's out there with a shotgun. And my HAND HURTS, MAX!!!

MAX. OK, OK. Calm down!

NICOLE. Let's go *now!*

MAX. We can't go home now. We need gas.

NICOLE. Just pay whatever we have to pay. Sell whatever we have to sell.

MAX. But we don't know what's going on back home. Maybe they're in a blackout too? We haven't seen a newspaper, heard a radio, nothing for six days. We can't just go back. Not yet.

NICOLE. So we just stay here for what? Another week? A month? Two months? A year?

MAX. Don't be ridiculous. This isn't going to last a month! *(Dogs barking off.)*

NICOLE. Why aren't the phones working, Max? Why isn't there any news?

MAX. Someone said they saw some National Guardsmen. So they'll tell us what to do.

NICOLE. Will they? Max, maybe they've been lying all along because they don't want people to panic, to make trouble. They're trying to control this situation. Maybe that's why the soldiers are here.

MAX. Who's "they"?

NICOLE. The people in charge. The government. "Homeland Security"! Do you think for a second, if something really bad happened, that they would want us to know about it? You think if there was some kind of massive terrorist attack they would let us in on it? THEY DON'T WANT US TO KNOW!

MAX. Nicole! Nicole! You're being paranoid. You have to get a grip on yourself.

NICOLE. But Max, admit it's a possibility!

MAX. OK, look, if by some wild stretch of the imagination something *has* happened out there, it's the last place on earth I want to be. And ... and ... We *don't* know. No one knows. Do you? I mean ... look, we get out on the road and there's no telling what we'll run into. It's all strangers out there.

NICOLE. It's all strangers *here,* Max. We don't know anybody *here.* We're totally cut off. No phones. No one's taking credit cards. And what happens when we run out of cash? When we run out of food?

MAX. We'll cross that bridge when we get to it.

NICOLE. We're crossing the bridge now! Right now! We are on the bridge and the bridge is very rickety and scary. Don't you see that?

MAX. No! Don't be so dramatic. I'm just trying to figure out the best way ...

NICOLE. *Fuck* the best way. This isn't something you take a poll on! You have to be decisive. Because I'll tell you something, in case you don't know ... This "situation" is not a stable situation. There are men at checkpoints. *Men.* With guns. And when men get together, shitty things happen.

MAX. Give it two more days.

NICOLE. Don't you care what happens to us? Or could happen to *me?* Aren't you afraid?

MAX. No, because I refuse to panic.

NICOLE. Max, being smart doesn't count around here. Whether you like it or not. This isn't Scrabble. This is a whole different rule book. *(Beat.)* Two more days, two more weeks. It's only going to get worse.

MAX. No. You're wrong. I know you're wrong. *(Nat appears in the mud room carrying a carton and a shotgun. He tries the door and finds it locked. He taps lightly. Max opens the door for him.)*

NAT. Good idea locking the door.

MAX. You been hunting, Nat? We heard a gun.

NAT. Not me.

MAX. But ... *(Indicating shotgun.)*

NAT. Oh, uh, No, this is my dad's. I don't know, seems to make sense to carry it. I can leave it in the truck if it bothers you.

MAX. No. It's fine. (*Nat props the shotgun up against the wall. Nicole goes back to the table and sits. Nat puts the carton he's carrying on the table, then pours himself a glass of cider.*)

NAT. So … How we all doin'? Hanging in there?

MAX. I could use a hot shower, but we seem to be OK. (*Nicole laughs sarcastically, as in "speak for yourself."*)

NAT. Zeke sent over some more eggs. And my mom threw in some of her canned beets. A loaf of bread. Candles. And clean water. I don't know how much of that pond water you should be drinking.

MAX. We boil it.

NAT. Guy in a truck was giving out all these unlabeled tins. Got to be something good in there. But if it smells like tuna it's probably cat food.

NICOLE. You want to sit down, Nat?

NAT. No. Thanks. I'll just unpack this stuff. There's a meeting down by the firehouse. Folks from around here trying to figure out what we're going to do.

NICOLE. What are people saying?

NAT. Well, I met a guy yesterday who said he saw some National Guardsmen going by in trucks.

MAX. Yeah. We heard something about that. I guess that's a good thing, right?

NAT. You know what they say, "This too shall pass."

NICOLE. Is that what they say?

MAX. We need wood. (*Max takes a hurricane lantern and exits. Nat picks up the empty jug of hard cider.*)

NAT. My great-grandma's recipe.

NICOLE. Yes. Delicious. (*Beat.*) Must have been wonderful growing up here.

NAT. Kind of boring, actually. A lot of hard work for a kid. Up before school, milking. Shoveling cow shit. Sterilizing milk cans. Checking the feed. Shoveling more shit. I hated shoveling shit.

NICOLE. But it must have been kind of peaceful.

NAT. You ever try to shove a cow through a lye bath? Nothing peaceful about a half ton of meat trying to kick your skull in.

NICOLE. Your family had a farm?

NAT. Used to. Belonged to my great-grandpa. Had twelve kids, but a bunch of 'em got the flu after World War I and died. They're all buried over in Waterville. One of the gravestones just says

"Baby," never even had a name.

NICOLE. "Baby"?

NAT. Yup. She would have been my mom's auntie I guess, if she had lived. But she didn't.

NICOLE. A baby with no name. That is so sad.

NAT. This is gonna sound silly, but every once in a while, I put flowers on the grave.

NICOLE. Do you have a girlfriend, Nat?

NAT. No. Not really.

NICOLE. You should. You're a nice man.

NAT. *(Smiling.)* You think so? *(Nicole pours herself cider and sips it.)*

NICOLE. You must think we're a bunch of assholes.

NAT. No, of course not.

NICOLE. You do. *(Nicole starts to cry. Nat isn't sure at first what she's doing and then when he does he's not sure how he should react.)*

NAT. Uh … *(Nat approaches Nicole, wanting to console her. Finally he pats her shoulder. She touches his hand. A moment. Nothing is said. Finally, Nicole pulls away from him and wipes her nose. Stands and gathers herself.)*

NICOLE. I'm sorry. *(Blowing her nose, etc.)* Look at me. In the city they call me the dragon-lady. *(Nat notices her awkwardness with her hand.)*

NAT. How's your hand?

NICOLE. It hurts. They told me I had to go back to the hospital, but I'm afraid they're going to tell me that it's infected. It hurts … a lot. *(Nicole holds back from crying again. Nat takes Nicole's hand and examines it.)*

NAT. No, no. It's not that bad, but you haven't been taking care of it. These stitches have to come out.

NICOLE. I know, we were supposed to go to the hospital two days ago. But I'm afraid …

NAT. Don't need the hospital. Here. *(Nat takes out his utility knife, pours vodka on it to clean it, runs it over the candle flame.)* Just look the other way for a second. *(Nat cuts each stitch and pulls it out.)* That'll be better now. Not that bad … Now, just hold on a sec, this will sting. *(He pours alcohol on the wound. Nicole winces, small sob.)* Then put this on. *(He applies ointment.)* In a few days it will heal up. OK? *(Nat holds her hand. Nicole weeps. We can hear Max chopping outside.)* Hey, everything's going to be fine. You're just scared that's all.

NICOLE. I don't know what I am. I feel light-headed and weak behind my knees all the time. Is that what fear feels like?

NAT. You have to have a little faith in people.

NICOLE. Yeah. *(Beat.)* Would you like some tea, Nat?

NAT. Love some. *(A stillness pervades. It is broken by Max, who enters with an armload of wood.)*

MAX. Should get us through the night.

NICOLE. Nat took care of my hand.

MAX. He did?

NICOLE. It feels much better.

MAX. Oh. Thanks, Nat.

NAT. I guess I should get going. *(Nat stands. Nicole grabs his arm and stops him.)*

NICOLE. No, sit down. Don't go.

MAX. Nat has to go to his meeting, Nicole.

NICOLE. I know. But after the meeting, could you come back here, Nat? *(Beat.)* Could you do that, Nat? Stay here tonight. We have the room.

NAT. I dunno. I guess.

NICOLE. Thank you. That would be good.

NAT. OK. Well, then I guess I'll see you later. *(Nat goes out to his truck.)*

MAX. Nicole, what are you doing? You're my wife, for God's sake!

NICOLE. "Wife"? What a strange word.

MAX. It's not strange. It's what you are.

NICOLE. Like something out of a nineteenth-century novel. "He had a wife." Which means what?

MAX. It means we're partners. "For better or worse. Sickness and health." You and me.

NICOLE. I guess.

MAX. Nicole, I understand if you're frightened. But this is an extraordinary situation.

NICOLE. Yeah? Maybe this is not an extraordinary situation. Maybe this is the norm. And maybe this is the real you and the real me, you know? Here in this place. Maybe our "normal" lives, *that's* extraordinary. Artificial.

MAX. But I mean, Nat. He's been very helpful, but we don't really know him. And you've seen the way he looks at you. You're encouraging him. I just don't understand, you want him to *stay* here?

NICOLE. I feel safe when he's around.

MAX. But he's going to think he belongs here.

NICOLE. He belongs here more than we do.

MAX. So what, he's going to live with us now?

NICOLE. Sure. Like you say, it's only going to be a couple of days.

MAX. This is so fucked up!

NICOLE. Oh, you're just realizing that?

MAX. Nicole! Don't you care about *my* feelings on this?

NICOLE. Max, I can't worry about how you "feel" right now.

MAX. Yeah, well that's the way it always is, isn't it?

NICOLE. No! It's not.

MAX. What *you* want, what *you* need. What *you* feel. You want a career — you work 24/7. You want a baby — suddenly you've got time for sex. Suddenly you have time for a vacation. You feel insecure — you invite a stranger into the house. It's the Nicole show. It's always been the Nicole show. I do what *you* want to do when *you* want to do it. What I want never figures into it.

NICOLE. What you want? Gee and who's been paying the bills for the last seven years so the great artist could have time to write? So *you* could have that luxury? So *you* could hang out all day and ponder the meaning of the universe?

MAX. I write because I have to.

NICOLE. And I have to work because you have to write.

MAX. I had no idea I was such a burden!

NICOLE. No, no. I had no idea living with me was so difficult. Sorry.

MAX. So now what?

NICOLE. I look at it this way, they give you lemons, make lemonade.

MAX. I hate lemonade.

NICOLE. Well you better to learn to like it, Max, 'cause there's nothing else to drink.

Scene 3

Lights brighten, dawn of a dark gloomy day. Washing has been hung across the space. We see that Nat's clothes are hung along with Max and Nicole's. Max, with a blanket wrapped around him, is squatting by the fire, poking at it. The door to one of the bedrooms above opens. Nat comes out, goes to the bathroom. Nat comes out of the bathroom and makes his way downstairs. He's wearing pieces of Max's clothing.

NAT. Morning.

MAX. Hmm. *(Beat.)*

NAT. I'm making breakfast, you want any? Eggs, hash browns?

MAX. Breakfast. No, that's OK. I'm fine. *(Nat busies himself in the kitchen, peeling and slicing potatoes.)*

NAT. Looks like you got that snow you wanted. More coming, either today or tonight.

MAX. Snow?

NAT. And I'll tell you. When it snows up here, it *snows*. *(Nat begins to whistling softly to himself. He's happy.)*

MAX. It gets dark early up here.

NAT. Oh yeah. The nights are long this time of year.

MAX. Now I understand why prehistoric people worshipped the sun. Must be what it's like around the polar circle. There's something sad about darkness. I guess because the dark is equated with death, with emptiness, with nothingness.

NAT. You know what? You think too much.

MAX. You're part of something, something large and stable. A world. *(Laughs.)* And suddenly it's eclipsed and that's frightening.

NAT. You think too much and you talk a lot.

MAX. I have to think. It's habit of mine. *(Nat comes and sits with Max, peeling potatoes.)*

NAT. Look, things haven't changed *that* much. In fact, things haven't changed much at all. The world's still out there. I'm still me, you're still you. We're healthy. We have a roof over our heads.

MAX. That simple, is it?

NAT. Why not?

MAX. See, back in the city, things aren't the same as up here. They're more ... complicated. It's not enough to stay warm and get fed. There's other kinds of sustenance. Of the mind, of the soul. A life. I have a life back there. I miss it. I know it doesn't mean anything to you, but I write, my work is published. OK? People all over the country have read my work. My work is admired. I've won awards. I know this sounds ridiculous, but back in the city, I *am* somebody.

NAT. Yeah? Have you ever been on a talk show?

MAX. Once.

NAT. I'm impressed.

MAX. I'm a writer. That's all.

NAT. When I was in high school, I had a friend who was a writer. Used to tell these great stories. Funny guy.

MAX. It's not the same thing.

NAT. Why not?

MAX. *(Standing.)* Where's Nicole? Why isn't she coming down?

NAT. I know this is going to sound like a dumb question, but if you're a writer how come I never see you do any writing? *(Max has no answer.)*

MAX. NICOLE?! *(Nicole wanders out of the bedroom.)* You're up early. *(Nicole ignores Max.)*

NAT. I'm making eggs, you want some?

NICOLE. Eggs? Sure. Why not? *(Nicole watches Nat as he cooks. Max addresses Nicole.)*

MAX. Last night I dreamt I was back in the city. Of all the places to dream about, I dreamt I was in a Starbucks. Can you believe that? How trite is that? Cappuccino as metaphor.

NAT. That's funny.

MAX. So I'm drinking a latte. Eating a freshly baked raisin scone and I'm buttering it, very thinly, but perfectly with perfect fresh butter. And I have the *Times* spread out in front of me and I'm trying to decide which half of the scone to eat first and then I hear this *beeping*. It was my beeper. I'd forgotten that I have an appointment. It's getting louder and louder.

NAT. Nicole, excuse me ... How do you like your eggs scrambled? Dry or soft?

NICOLE. Soft.

NAT. Hash browns?

NICOLE. Yum!

MAX. Never mind.

NICOLE. What Max? We're listening. Keep going. Your beeper's getting louder, yeah.

NAT. What happened?

MAX. So uh … in the dream … I'm very late. For my appointment. And it's getting dark outside but I haven't finished my coffee. I take a sip, I burn my tongue. I haven't eaten my scone. I haven't even read the first section of the *Times*. I *need* to read the *Times*. There's a cyclone off the coast of Calcutta I need to know about. But I'm late, so I run out into the street. And there's no street lights. Everything's dark. And people are running and I'm running with them. We're all running in the darkness. Because we're all late. And then I realize I forgot my Palm Pilot at the Starbucks and I turn back to get it, but I can't find the Starbucks anymore. I panic. Without my Palm Pilot, what will happen to me? You know? I was running out of time … and I was … late.

NAT. And the moral of the story is?

MAX. No moral. It's just interesting the way I see myself in my dreams.

NICOLE. Seems pretty accurate.

MAX. No it's not! I don't have a beeper. I hate scones. I don't even own a Palm Pilot!

NAT. The moral of the story is always give yourself enough time.

MAX. No!

NAT. Watch out for hot coffee? You might burn your tongue? *(Nicole laughs.)*

MAX. Sorry I brought it up.

NAT. The Wal-Mart got looted. *(Beat. Max goes to the fire and dicks with it. Restacks the wood.)* The state police are starting a curfew.

NICOLE. Why?

NAT. Well, you know, this kind of situation, some people have difficulty behaving themselves.

MAX. Running low on wood.

NAT. Hey Max, that reminds me, good news! Slim's gonna sell me a generator. I can hook it right up to the house and we can have lights in here. I might even be able to get the oil burner started. *(Max says nothing, keeps stacking. Nat brings a plate of food to Nicole.)* And I was thinking, you and I might want to get up on the roof today, take a look at the gutters, make sure everything is tight before more snow comes. And we should put up some deer fencing. Because if we don't get more snow today, we definitely will tomorrow, definitely. *(Nicole has buttered some bread and brought it to Max. But he doesn't touch it. He doesn't look up.)* Oh, and I almost forgot! My mom's

cousin has a whole cellar full of acorn squash he's just been throwin' to his hogs. Says we can have all we can eat. How 'bout that? A little maple syrup and butter, acorn squash is good. *(Max is obsessively stacking and restacking the firewood.)*
NICOLE. Max, please stop doing that and have something to eat.
MAX. I have to get this wood stacked.
NAT. You sure you don't want any of this? You don't know what you're missing.
NICOLE. It is good.
NAT. No brag, just fact. *(Nicole and Nat laugh. Max gets up to leave the room.)*
NICOLE. Where are you going?
MAX. I have things to do.
NICOLE. What do you have to do?
MAX. I have to write. *(Max leaves.)*

Scene 4

Night. Max sits at a table alone, writing by a Coleman lamp. He is unaware of the passing headlights that can be seen flashing by outside. Spoon enters. She looks tired.

SPOON. Hi.
MAX. Spoon? My god.
SPOON. You look like you've seen a ghost.
MAX. It's been two weeks.
SPOON. Yeah. Well.
MAX. Are you OK?
SPOON. Sort of. Yeah.
MAX. I'm so happy to see you.
SPOON. I just came to get my stuff. I didn't think you'd be up.
MAX. I don't sleep much at the moment. I have a lot of work to do.
SPOON. It's three in the morning.
MAX. Actually, I don't sleep at all.
SPOON. You're writing?
MAX. Yes.
SPOON. You haven't heard from ...

MAX. No … We thought maybe you guys found each other.

SPOON. No.

MAX. No. He's probably in Chicago by now. *(Max picks up the lantern and holds it up to Spoon. Her face is dirty.)* So … What happened to you?

SPOON. Nothing. Everything's fine.

MAX. Oh.

SPOON. I ran into a little trouble. But everything's OK now. *(Max notices headlights for the first time.)*

MAX. Is there someone out there?

SPOON. Yeah. A guy I met. Trucker.

MAX. Doesn't he want to come in?

SPOON. No.

MAX. Did he do this to you?

SPOON. No. He … he … *(Spoon begins to cry …)*

MAX. Oh …

SPOON. I got really hungry, you know? And so I found this cabin that had a freezer. And I found this frozen lasagna. And those potato puffs you just heat up in the oven. And a bottle of wine. It was so nice, it was almost normal. The only thing that was missing was a VCR. I had a little buzz from the wine and I guess I fell asleep. And then … there was all this bright light, through the windows … incredibly bright ugly light. And there was all this pounding on the door. Like explosions. And then these men were all in the room with me. They were pulling me and grabbing at me, making me stand up. And I got angry and pushed one of them away. And someone hit me.

MAX. God.

SPOON. I woke up and they were gone. Just one guy. My friend. He'd been protecting me. Keeping them away from me. He's got a truck and he's going to give me a ride.

MAX. To where?

SPOON. North. He's going North. I'm going with him. He said he heard that the lights are on in Canada. *(Spoon begins to go to her room. Max stands up.)*

MAX. Your things. Your things aren't in there. I put them … here … *(Max finds Spoon's things and gets them for her.)*

SPOON. Oh thanks.

MAX. You sure you're OK?

SPOON. No. Are you sure *you're* OK?

MAX. No.

SPOON. Well, at least you're writing. That's good.

MAX. Last night, I woke up and the place was so cold. Like ice. The fire had gone out. So I went out to collect some kindling. And I found myself standing in the middle of the field. No moon. Pitch-dark. Freezing. The stars, so intense, piercing the sky. They were so much brighter because there was no other light.

SPOON. No moon last night.

MAX. No. And as I was watching the sky, must have been for fifteen minutes, I realized I hadn't seen one jet go over. Not one. So I waited. Freezing. I waited to see one jet. One red light blinking. I stood there for a long time and I didn't see one. The sky was just a giant vacuum, black and still. I felt so small. So anonymous. And I thought, I want to be back home. I want to be me again. This way, I'm not me. And if anything happened, if I were to get stuck up here, no one would ever find out. I'd just disappear, my whole life would disappear — all the things I've done, my work, my dreams — and no one would ever know I had ever lived.

SPOON. Yeah.

MAX. Like people who die in a plague. Who die in some enormous disaster. Who were they? Who knows their names? Where are the bodies? No one really knows. If you die anonymously, does that mean you were never alive in the first place?

SPOON. I shouldn't keep my friend waiting.

MAX. No. *(She starts to go.)* Spoon. It means a lot to me that you liked my story.

SPOON. It was a wonderful story. You're a wonderful writer.

MAX. Yes. I need to write. The new work is good. The best I've ever done. I'd print out some pages for you to take, but there's no printer. Wouldn't be able to plug it in if there was. I'm writing longhand for the first time in years.

SPOON. But that's good.

MAX. Yeah. I suppose it is. You better go. We'll all get together the next time ... well, whenever.

SPOON. Bye. *(Spoon leaves. Max goes to back to writing.)*

55

Scene 5

Max is working on a legal pad by the fire. Nat and Nicole are at the large oak table, setting up a Scrabble game. The place is much neater.

NICOLE. Max. Come on.

NAT. Yeah Max, I'd figure you'd be pretty good at this.

MAX. I'm working.

NAT. *(Into the game.)* There you go! C-L-O-C-K! Double letter on the "K," plus double word!

NICOLE. Plus you crossed the other word, so you get the double word there too! That's ... *(Counting.)* ... forty-seven! Wow! *(Laughing.)*

NAT. I guess I got the knack.

MAX. Hey Nat, don't eggs come from chickens? How 'bout your buddy Zeke sends over a couple of chickens? Or slaughter one of those dairy cows? A nice thick steak would be a welcome change of pace.

NAT. *(With a chuckle.)* Well, I wouldn't feel right asking him to do anything like that.

MAX. You wouldn't feel right?

NAT. Nope.

MAX. You know what, Jethro? I don't give a shit what you feel right doing. You're supposed to be taking care of this place, you're supposed to be taking care of *us*. And it seems to me you're doing a pretty *shitty* job of it. There's no heat. All we have to eat are eggs. You can't even find me a newspaper. *(Max zeroes in on them.)* Seems like you've got things all mixed up. This is my vacation, not yours.

NICOLE. *(Focusing on the scrabble.)* If I could use that "K," I'd be in business. What starts with "K"?

MAX. *(Still on Nat.)* You work for me.

NICOLE. "Krispy Kreme"? *(Nat and Nicole laugh. Neither looks up at Max.)*

MAX. Gee, you and my wife are getting to be such good friends! Who knows? You hang around long enough, might get lucky, huh?

NICOLE. Max, that's enough.

MAX. *(To Nat:)* Don't see too many women like her up this way, do you? A real prize. Doesn't smoke. Literate. Has all her teeth. A little skinny, maybe, but feed her enough eggs, she'll fatten up.

NAT. *(Staring hard at his Scrabble tiles.)* You can shuttup now.

MAX. I don't have to shuttup. That's my wife. This is *my* house. Fuck you.

NAT. You're mistaken, friend. This was never your house.

MAX. Yeah? Well, just remember this, *pal,* she's quite a piece of ass, but it comes at a price. You're gonna have to rake a lot of leaves to keep her in style.

NAT. *(Standing, in Max's face.)* You better stop.

MAX. You gonna hit me? Huh? Right. Go clean out a gutter. *(Slap! Nat cuffs Max in the face, knocking him back.)*

NICOLE. Oh, Max! *(Nat stands his ground. Clenches his fist. Max says nothing. Holding his face, sulks back to his writing.)*

NAT. I warned him. You heard me. You heard me warn him. *(Nat sits down and stares at the tiles. Big silence all around.)* Damn. I forgot what word I was thinking of. *(Nicole goes to Max, not getting too close.)*

NICOLE. *(To Max.)* This is … Max … why do you have to make everything so … are you OK?

NAT. I didn't hurt him. Just gave him a little tap. *(Pointing at Max.)* I warned you. You can't say I didn't warn you. But no, you just can't stop talking can you? Gotta push it. Talking off the top of your head. Even if it's about your own wife. If I hadn't a smacked you, who knows what woulda come out a your mouth next? Look — I don't mind that you people are a spoiled bunch. I figure you can't help yourselves. It's the way you people are, you come from someplace far from here. And I don't expect to understand. But when you cross the line, and let me tell you, I've been patient, but when you cross that line, I just say to myself, they're like children and children have to be spanked every now and then. *(As Nat continues, Max moves away from Nicole, goes to the kitchen, gets a glass of water.)* I don't want to be the one to do it. But I'll tell you, *sir,* and I'll tell you straight, you are not back in the big bad city, you're not back where everyone does and says whatever the hell they feel like. You're on my turf. And when you're on *my* turf, you better behave yourself. Or you're gonna get what's coming to you. *(Beat.)* Now. Behave yourself and we'll all get along fine. That's all I have to say. *(Max, in the kitchen, addresses Nat.)*

MAX. Nat. You always have a full tank of gas. I know you know where to get it. Gimme half your tank and we'll get out of here.

57

NAT. You don't want to do that.

MAX. Why not?

NAT. It's just not a good idea, Max. Nothing but trouble out there. Bikers. Crazies.

MAX. Fuck the bikers. We want to leave.

NAT. But where would you go?

MAX. That's my business isn't it?

NAT. Listen. I have taken care of you guys all along. And despite what you think, I like you. So take it easy and in a few days, maybe a week, things will probably be looking up. We'll fix your heat. We'll get some supplies in. It'll be fine. We're all gonna be fine.

MAX. We're not going to be fine. Nicole isn't fine. I'm not fine. We're leaving.

NAT. Max, why don't you sit down and calm down? *(Nat comes over to console Max. Max backs away and steps into ... Nat's shotgun. Max grabs it and cocks it.)*

MAX. Back off.

NICOLE. Max, what are you doing?

MAX. Nat's going to give us gas and we're going to leave. Right now.

NAT. Please put my shotgun down. *(Nat steps toward Max.)* Mister, that's my gun and I want you to put it down. I don't like it when people touch my stuff.

NICOLE. Max, stop it.

NAT. You don't know what you're doin'. Gimme. *(Nat steps a bit closer to Max. Max is pointing the gun at Nat.)*

MAX. This is a gun.

NAT. Uh-huh. *(Nat relents, drops his hands.)*

MAX. We're leaving. Nicole, go get your stuff. We'll take his truck. He's got a full tank, I know he does.

NICOLE. No.

MAX. No?

NICOLE. No. *(Max grabs her wrist, tries to move her toward the door.)*

MAX. Yes! We can get to Canada. We can. *(Nicole breaks away, almost hysterical.)*

NICOLE. Max! There's nowhere to go! OK? Isn't that obvious? It's too dangerous. You told me what happened to Spoon. God! Out there, out there ... I can't!!!

MAX. This is what you wanted!

NICOLE. No. Not anymore. Not now. *(Nicole turns away from Max and crouches down, shaking with fear. She can't face him.)* If you're doing this for me, don't, because I can't come with you. I won't come with you.

MAX. No?

NICOLE. I'm sorry.

NAT. Max, why don't you go upstairs and lie down?

MAX. I don't want to lie down. I want … I want to … I need to … *(Crying.)* Shit!

NICOLE. Max, what are you doing? Stop it!

MAX. *(Steels himself.)* It's just … it's just this can't be what we think it is. It can't. It's not possible. Nicole, look at me. I'm your *husband*. I love you. You love me. We have to go. You and me. Right now.

NAT. Like she said. Go rest. You'll feel better tomorrow. *(Max turns the gun on Nat.)*

MAX. SHUTTUP. JUST SHUTTUP! This has nothing to do with you!

NICOLE. I'm sorry, Max.

MAX. Stop saying you're sorry! Nicole, it's OK. We're going to get out of here and what happens happens. We just need each other, right? NICOLE! Look at me!

NICOLE. I *can't* Max. Don't make me. *(Max lets the gun droop. Nat jumps forward, grabs the barrel, pushes it aside and pulls it away. The gun goes off. Nat grabs his inner thigh and falls onto the floor.)*

NAT. Ahhhh! You shot me!

NICOLE. Oh God! What did you do, Max?!

NAT. I'm bleeding! Goddamnit! Ahhhh!!!

NICOLE. You shot him, Max!

MAX. No I didn't. It went off!

NAT. Damn! I told you to leave it alone! Now look what you did. My leg … Jesus!

MAX. No, it's … uh … let's put something on it. Wrap it. *(Max runs over to the hanging clothes and grabs a shirt. He rushes back to Nat.)*

NAT. Lotta blood.

MAX. Yeah, OK.

NICOLE. Max!

NAT. I don't feel so good.

MAX. Just a sec. There.

NAT. I feel sleepy.

MAX. No, don't go to sleep! Shit, I can't find the wound. *(Pause. Nat closes his eyes. Lies back.)*

NICOLE. What's he doing? Is he breathing?

MAX. Yes. But I can't … the blood …

NICOLE. But Max, what are we going to do?

MAX. I don't know. I don't know.

NICOLE. Is he going to die?

MAX. No!

NICOLE. He is.

MAX. Nicole. Stop.

NICOLE. He's still bleeding. Look.

MAX. I can see that. I don't know, Michelle. *(Slaps Nat.)* Wake up. Wake up, Nat. *(Pause. Nothing happens. Max is feeling Nat's throat for a pulse.)*

MAX. He's alive. I think. *(The lights flicker and then illuminate. The stereo begins to play. Water begins to flow from the taps. No one says anything. The phone begins to ring. Max steps back into the house. No one moves. The answering machine clicks on.)*

ANSWERING MACHINE VOICE. *(Woman's voice.)* Hello, this is Ted and Sondra. *(Guy's voice:)* Hi! *(Woman:)* We're not here right now, so leave a message. If not, have a great 24/7!

BILLY'S VOICE. Nicole? Are you there? I've had you on autodial forever! Are you guys alright? *(Nicole grabs the phone.)*

NICOLE. *(To phone:)* Billy? … Yeah, yeah, hey! No. Uh, we had, you know, some problems, in fact things have been very … what? … oh … well, that's great. That's wonderful. *(Listening.)* You know what? Umm, can I call you back? No, I will. In a little while. Let me call you back, OK, Billy? Thanks hon. *(Nicole gently puts the phone back in its cradle.)* Billy says the blackout's over. *(The lights get brighter. No one moves. The lights become overwhelmingly bright. Blackout.)*

End of Play

PROPERTY LIST

Cell phones
Luggage
Groceries/various food items
Plates, silverware, etc.
Scrabble
Wine bottles
Drinking glasses
Case of books (MAX)
Laptop computer (MAX)
Note (MAX)
Box of records (NICOLE)
Paper (MAX, TROY)
Wood (MAX)
Matches (MAX, SPOON)
Jacket (NICOLE)
Shirt (MAX)
Wrenches (MAX)
Cooler (NAT)
Palm Pilot (TROY)
Dictionary (SPOON)
Flashlight (MAX)
Candles (SPOON)
Coleman lamp (NAT, MAX)
Pans (NAT)
Bowls (NAT)
Car keys (MAX)
Bottle of Stoli (TROY, SPOON)
Coal scuttle full of pine cones (SPOON)
Joint (TROY)
Jugs of water (NAT)
Yellow pages (NICOLE)
Stage blood (NICOLE)
White towel (NICOLE)
Axe (MAX)
Plastic jug of hard cider (SPOON)
Tea kettle (NICOLE)
TV (TROY)
Boxes (TROY)
Cigarette (SPOON)

Jacket (SPOON)
Coat (MAX)
Paper towels (MAX)
Carton (NAT)
Shotgun (NAT)
Hurricane lantern (NAT)
Utility knife (NAT)
Ointment (NAT)
Blanket (MAX)
Potato peeler (NAT)
Pen or pencil (MAX)
Legal pad (MAX)

SOUND EFFECTS

Chickadee chirping
Phone ringing
Answering machine voice-overs
Sound of wood being split
Dogs barking
Sound of gun being fired

NEW PLAYS

★ **INTIMATE APPAREL by Lynn Nottage.** The moving and lyrical story of a turn-of-the-century black seamstress whose gifted hands and sewing machine are the tools she uses to fashion her dreams from the whole cloth of her life's experiences. "…Nottage's play has a delicacy and eloquence that seem absolutely right for the time she is depicting…" –*NY Daily News.* "…thoughtful, affecting…The play offers poignant commentary on an era when the cut and color of one's dress—and of course, skin—determined whom one could and could not marry, sleep with, even talk to in public." –*Variety.* [2M, 4W] ISBN: 0-8222-2009-1

★ **BROOKLYN BOY by Donald Margulies.** A witty and insightful look at what happens to a writer when his novel hits the bestseller list. "The characters are beautifully drawn, the dialogue sparkles…" –*nytheatre.com.* "Few playwrights have the mastery to smartly investigate so much through a laugh-out-loud comedy that combines the vintage subject matter of successful writer-returning-to-ethnic-roots with the familiar mid-life crisis." –*Show Business Weekly.* [4M, 3W] ISBN: 0-8222-2074-1

★ **CROWNS by Regina Taylor.** Hats become a springboard for an exploration of black history and identity in this celebratory musical play. "Taylor pulls off a Hat Trick: She scores thrice, turning CROWNS into an artful amalgamation of oral history, fashion show, and musical theater…" –*TheatreMania.com.* "…wholly theatrical…Ms. Taylor has created a show that seems to arise out of spontaneous combustion, as if a bevy of department-store customers simultaneously decided to stage a revival meeting in the changing room." –*NY Times.* [1M, 6W (2 musicians)] ISBN: 0-8222-1963-8

★ **EXITS AND ENTRANCES by Athol Fugard.** The story of a relationship between a young playwright on the threshold of his career and an aging actor who has reached the end of his. "[Fugard] can say more with a single line than most playwrights convey in an entire script…Paraphrasing the title, it's safe to say this drama, making its memorable entrance into our consciousness, is unlikely to exit as long as a theater exists for exceptional work." –*Variety.* "A thought-provoking, elegant and engrossing new play…" –*Hollywood Reporter.* [2M] ISBN: 0-8222-2041-5

★ **BUG by Tracy Letts.** A thriller featuring a pair of star-crossed lovers in an Oklahoma City motel facing a bug invasion, paranoia, conspiracy theories and twisted psychological motives. "…obscenely exciting…top-flight craftsmanship. Buckle up and brace yourself…" –*NY Times.* "…[a] thoroughly outrageous and thoroughly entertaining play…the possibility of enemies, real and imagined, to squash has never been more theatrical." –*A.P.* [3M, 2W] ISBN: 0-8222-2016-4

★ **THOM PAIN (BASED ON NOTHING) by Will Eno.** An ordinary man muses on childhood, yearning, disappointment and loss, as he draws the audience into his last-ditch plea for empathy and enlightenment. "It's one of those treasured nights in the theater—treasured nights anywhere, for that matter—that can leave you both breathless with exhilaration and…in a puddle of tears." –*NY Times.* "Eno's words…are familiar, but proffered in a way that is constantly contradictory to our expectations. Beckett is certainly among his literary ancestors." –*nytheatre.com.* [1M] ISBN: 0-8222-2076-8

★ **THE LONG CHRISTMAS RIDE HOME by Paula Vogel.** Past, present and future collide on a snowy Christmas Eve for a troubled family of five. "…[a] lovely and hauntingly original family drama…a work that breathes so much life into the theater." –*Time Out.* "…[a] delicate visual feast…" –*NY Times.* "…brutal and lovely…the overall effect is magical." –*NY Newsday.* [3M, 3W] ISBN: 0-8222-2003-2

DRAMATISTS PLAY SERVICE, INC.
440 Park Avenue South, New York, NY 10016 212-683-8960 Fax 212-213-1539
postmaster@dramatists.com   www.dramatists.com